Playing the Devil's Game

Playing the Devil's Game

CATHLYN DORÉ LAW and BECKI ROGERS

Pacific Press® Publishing Association
Nampa, Idaho | www.pacificpress.com

Cover design by Steve Lanto
Cover design resources from iStockphoto.com
Inside design by Aaron Troia

Copyright © 2021 by Pacific Press® Publishing Association
Printed in the United States of America
All rights reserved

The author assumes full responsibility for the accuracy of all facts and quotations as cited in this book.

All Bible texts are from the New King James Version®. Copyright © 1982 by Thomas Nelson. Used by permission. All rights reserved.

You can obtain additional copies of this book by calling toll-free 1-800-765-6955 or by visiting http://www.adventistbookcenter.com.

Library of Congress Cataloging-in-Publication Data

Names: Law, Cathy, author. | Rogers, Becki, author.
Title: Playing the devil's game / Cathy Law and Becki Rogers.
Description: Nampa, Idaho : Pacific Press Publishing Association, [2020] | Includes bibliographical references. | Summary: "Becki's story of God rescuing her from the occult"— Provided by publisher.
Identifiers: LCCN 2020036677 | ISBN 9780816366996 (paperback) | ISBN 9780816367009 (ebook)
Subjects: LCSH: Rogers, Becki. | Seventh-Day Adventist converts—United States—Biography. | Occultism—Religious aspects—Christianity. | Spiritualism.
Classification: LCC BX6189.R64 L39 2020 | DDC 286.7092 [B]—dc23
LC record available at https://lccn.loc.gov/2020036677

January 2021

Contents

A Word From Me to You		7
1	Ouija Nightmare	9
2	"Satan, If You're Here . . ."	17
3	Truth or Fiction?	25
4	Experiences or the Bible?	33
5	Discoveries	41
6	Night Attack	49
7	Prayer Panic	55
8	Not a Circus	63
9	Death Is Waiting	71
10	Divine Encounter	79
11	The Ultimate Decision	87
12	A Test of Faith	95
13	Satan's Countermove	103
14	Faith Wins	109
15	Unexpected Love	117

A Word From Me to You

Have you felt Jesus tugging at your heart? Maybe you have struggled with understanding the Bible or you don't understand occult issues. Or maybe you're not sure where you stand with God. There's a reason you are holding this book in your hands. I think God wanted you to read this book. Not only for you to see what He's done in my life but also for you to discover His love for you. If I could say only one thing to you, I'd say, "God is *real*, and His love for you is so sincere and intense it's hard to comprehend."

I promise you, there is hope for everyone. Jesus, who has saved my life physically, healed me emotionally, and helped me spiritually, is waiting with open arms to welcome you into a new life!

Won't you experience Jesus for yourself through Bible study

and Christian fellowship? Heaven is real, and it's just around the corner. If you would like to know love like you've never experienced it before, you will find it in Jesus. The Bible says that God *is* love.

I encourage you to connect with your local Seventh-day Adventist pastor and allow him or her to guide you to the One who has a never-failing love for you. You'll not be sorry.

May God's peace, love, and blessings be with you always.

Becki Rogers

1

Ouija Nightmare

"Open the door! *Open the door!*" I recognized my kid sister Cindy's voice screaming above the persistent pounding of her fists at the front door. A friend and I had been deep into the thriller on TV, but it couldn't compare with what was going on back home at this very moment.

Swinging the door open, I found Cindy standing on the porch shaking her hands in helpless distraction. "Becki," she blurted, "you have to come home. Something's wrong with Mom!"

Not waiting for an explanation, I darted out the door. My mind shot in all directions searching the possibilities. *Heart attack? Accident?*

Breathless, I bounded up the steps of our house and rushed in. Mom's friend, Debbie, was sitting across the dining room table from her. Debbie's face was distorted with fear. Seeing me, she whispered to Randy, my older brother, "She's here." Though my family had come to regard me as a bit of a spiritual freak, there were times they appreciated my leanings toward God.

"What's going on?" I asked in bewilderment.

"The spirits are trying to get into Mom." DJ, my younger brother, stood staring at Mom as he spoke.

I saw the Ouija board in the center of the table.

It was nothing new in our home. Mom regularly played the game with friends and relatives. Many mornings I had seen little scraps of paper littering the coffee table where my aunt had jotted down answers Ouija had given them the night before.

As a youngster, I had been awakened one night by a rhythmic chant. Drawn downstairs by my curiosity, I had peeked into the dining room, where I saw Mom's friends and some of our relatives with their hands lightly resting on the table. In unison they were repeating, "Rise, table, rise," their voices increasing in volume to an urgent crescendo.

Though I wasn't quite sure what they were doing, the scene left me with a creepy feeling, so I tiptoed back upstairs wishing I had never seen it. But it was just a game, wasn't it?

However, this time the game had morphed into a nightmare.

"She's not breathing!" Debbie erupted with a scream. Trembling, she backed as far away from the Ouija board as she could, flattening herself against the wall.

"Get that candle," Randy snapped at DJ. Going to the counter, DJ brought the candle and a lighter to the table. The blackened wick showed that the candle had been lit before. Lighting the candle again, Randy held it directly in front of Mom's mouth.

"Watch. See, the flame doesn't even flicker," Randy said. He was right. There was no movement from Mom's chest to indicate she was breathing. Her eyes stared blankly into space. DJ pulled the candle away and put out the flame.

Then Randy said, "Watch this." Flicking his fingers close to Mom's face failed to bring even the slightest flinch from her. Coming close, he blew into her eyes. Again, no movement. "I've even thrown water into her face, and that's all we get!" He gestured toward Mom who looked more like a statue than a human. *What caused this?* My mind scrambled for an answer.

Debbie suddenly exclaimed, "Look!" Her finger pointed shakily at the heart-shaped message indicator on the Ouija board. Our eyes followed the moving device. Before coming to a stop, it cruised over the two rows of letters that arched in rainbow fashion across the board. We could see the needle clearly pointing at the letter *K* through the lens. Knowing the indicator would spell out a message, we watched uneasily.

DJ and I repeated the letters aloud as the indicator moved and stopped at each one: "*K...I...L...L....S...U...E.*"

I stared in disbelief at Mom's name. My heart was pounding. The message indicator continued: "Let me in.... I want your body.... KILL SUE!" This brought another scream from Debbie as she slid under the table like a cowering animal, putting her hands over her face in an effort to shut out the horrible drama.

"Becki, *do something!*" she pleaded hysterically.

This Ouija nightmare had been years in the making. My mom had grown up attending church with her mother. Then an aunt had introduced her at an early age to a new game: the Ouija board.

"It's just a game," Mom's aunt coaxed as she displayed the board and began to show Mom how to play it. Mom was intrigued with this new pastime. When she turned sixteen, her boyfriend gave her a gift.

"I made it myself," he said proudly as she admired his masterpiece. The homemade Ouija board was 14 inches by 18 inches with neat sapphire letters and numbers written in calligraphy. In each upper corner was a picture—a moon with the word *no* on one side and a sun with the word *yes* on the other.

"Let's ask Ouija some questions—any questions," he urged. "Let's see . . . I know. Will I graduate from high school?" Nothing happened for a moment. But then, as Mom rested her hand on the message indicator, it began to move. Bristling with excitement, they watched as it came to rest over the word *yes*.

"See!" Mom's boyfriend exclaimed triumphantly.

Mom was thrilled to have a Ouija board of her own. I don't know if Mom knew that the Bible clearly prohibited having anything to do with divination (Deuteronomy 18:10–12), but the Ouija game began Mom's lifetime fascination with the occult.

Mom eventually married her boyfriend. And with his gift of the Ouija board, she stepped into a spiritual realm she knew little of. It was a world that promised the entertaining excitement of communication with what she referred to as "the spirits." Neighbors and friends began to seek out Mom to get a peek into their futures. She enjoyed this new influence with people. It carried an appealing sense of control—a power—she had never known before.

Sadly, Mom's marriage ended when I was eight weeks old. During this time she had a nervous breakdown and was taken to the hospital. As an infant, I slept in Grandma and Grandpa's dresser drawer. After a few weeks, Mom recovered and was released from the hospital. Shortly after my first birthday, she married my stepdad.

When I was about five years old, we moved to another house. After getting the furniture in place, my parents went to bed. In the morning I wandered out to the living room and sat on the couch. About that time my dad came into the room, stretching and yawning. He stopped short, looking around the room.

Puzzled, he called out, "Hey, honey, why did you rearrange the furniture? I liked the couch over by the window."

Coming out of the bedroom, Mom asked, "What are you talking about? I didn't rearrange anything." Then she gazed around the room.

"Becki," Dad said as he turned to me, "did you move the furniture?"

Mom sniffed. "She's not strong enough to move all this furniture around. Besides, we would have heard it if she had done that."

Shaking his head, Dad started to put things back the way they had been the night before. Strangely, the next morning the furniture had been moved again. After this happened two more times, my mom gave up.

"OK, fine. If you want the furniture this way, I'll just leave it," Mom sighed. Looking at me, she said, "You know, Becki, I guess the spirit thinks it looks better this way." She shrugged and walked into the kitchen to fix breakfast. Mom was beginning to accept the presence of the spirits in our home as if they were harmless neighbors.

I, on the other hand, was not quite so trusting of them. One day, when I was a preschooler tagging along after Randy, we began exploring the garage, trying to find something to do. Spying a paintbrush, I picked it up. "We could finish painting the garage," I suggested.

"Nah." Randy shook his head. He well remembered the last time we'd attempted a paint job. We had mistakenly used black wheel-bearing grease instead of paint. It had created quite a mess, and Dad had been pretty upset.

I spotted a hammer. "Hey, we can pound some nails into a board," I enthused. "Wouldn't that be fun?"

"No." Randy waved off my idea. Then his eyes lit up as he pulled down a shovel. "Let's dig into hell and see what the devil *really* looks like," he said excitedly.

Now I was scared. "W-w-w-w-hat if that old devil gets mad at us?" I shivered at the thought. "I mean, he may not like us just dropping in while he's torturing people." It's hard to say where I had gotten such an idea of the devil and hell, but there were plenty of TV cartoons and horror movies to suggest such things.

Considering my objection, Randy picked up a hammer. "Here," he said, holding it out to me. "Take this and watch while I'm digging. If you see the devil coming out of the ground, smash him with this hammer." He made a fast pounding motion with his hand, showing me just what to do. "And then I'll throw dirt on him and stomp him back down into the ground." With considerable misgivings, I followed Randy's suggestion.

As Randy had instructed, I knelt on the grass, watching while he dug. My hand ached from the intense grip I had on the hammer, but I was thoroughly convinced that I would see those red, crooked fingers coming out of the ground to grab us at any moment.

When Randy was up to his knees in dirt, I asked, "Is it hot yet?"

Shaking his head, Randy kept digging. Though we persisted in this project for about two weeks, we never did hear tortured screams or moans from the pit.

As I grew older, I saw things in our home that shaped my understanding of the supernatural world that remain hidden to most people. I believed there was a devil, but I didn't understand his connection with the seemingly harmless spirits that were in our house.

One day Mom had visitors. Their talking and laughter drew me into the living room to see what I was missing. Aunt Ciara had just poured herself a cup of coffee. As she entered the living room where Uncle Reece was standing, I saw a spirit suddenly appear. He was tall and thin, wearing a long coat and hat. Reaching out, he took hold of Aunt Ciara's hand and poured her coffee onto the floor.

Dumbly, Uncle Reece and Aunt Ciara stood there. They didn't see the spirit, and he smiled as if he was enjoying his little joke. Then he disappeared.

"Why did I do that?" Aunt Ciara asked, baffled.

Uncle Reece shrugged his shoulders. "I don't know. Why *did* you do that?" They both laughed as Aunt Ciara went to get a towel to clean up the mess.

As Mom got acquainted with the neighbors, they told her that a man had died in our home before we moved in. So it was no surprise that they referred to it as a haunted house. This image was enhanced when, after we were all tucked into bed one night, a babysitter heard marbles being rolled across the room and rowdy kids jumping around in our bedroom. She hurried up the stairs to get us settled down only to find everyone sound asleep.

"Something's not right," she complained to my parents later. She never came back.

2

"Satan, If You're Here..."

Cindy and I shared a bedroom. She slept on a crib mattress on the floor. This way she could get in and out of bed by herself.

One night when I was about five years old, I awakened to see an old man sitting at the foot of Cindy's bed. He had a round, grandfatherly face, and he was tenderly gazing at her sleeping. He was wearing dress pants with cuffs, scuffed shoes, and a long overcoat. Tufts of gray hair were sticking out from under his hat.

I should have been afraid seeing a stranger in our bedroom at night, but he had become a familiar sight. His frequent visits were the result of my mom's decision to accept evil spirits into our home instead of heeding the Bible's warning to "have no fellowship with the unfruitful works of darkness" (Ephesians

5:11). Having no understanding of this myself, I wondered, *Why doesn't he ever sit on my bed?*

About that time, in the next room, Randy woke up wanting a drink of water. To get downstairs to the kitchen, he had to pass through the room where Cindy and I were sleeping. When Randy opened the door, I watched him stare momentarily at the old man. Suddenly the spirit jumped up and ran down the stairs. Randy took off after him. I lay in bed listening to their footsteps beneath me, darting around furniture, sometimes knocking something over. The next thing I knew, I heard them galloping up the stairs.

The old man appeared first and ran to the center of the room. Moving his hands as if opening an invisible curtain, he stepped through and disappeared into thin air!

Just then Randy ran into the room, panting. He stopped and looked around. "Are you looking for the old man?" I asked.

"Yes," he said anxiously. "Where did he go?"

When I told Randy how the old man had disappeared, he was incredulous.

"Becki, people don't just disappear. *Where did he go?*"

I described what I had seen. Randy came over and stood in front of me. I didn't know how to explain this other world that seemed to be in our world. But I was adamant. *The old man had disappeared.*

Giving up on my story, Randy checked to make sure Cindy was OK. He looked all around her mattress. He even peered into our closet, but there was no one there.

"People don't just disappear," he muttered. He went to

Mom's bed and shook her gently. Recounting the strange episode, he then said, "I saw a g-g-g-ghost!"

Half asleep and unshaken, Mom replied, "Good! Go ask him his name." With that, she sleepily turned over.

It was well known in the neighborhood that Mom advised people about the future based on answers she got from the Ouija board. One day when I came in from playing outside, I saw a man talking with Mom in the dining room.

"How did you know that?" he gasped. "I was alone when that happened. There is no way you could have known that!"

"I don't make up the answers," Mom laughed. "The spirits answer the questions."

Though Mom had chosen to make the occult a part of her life, Grandma took me to church with her a few times. I vaguely remember realizing that I needed to be quiet and listen in church.

I was also invited to go to church with a neighbor one Sunday morning. Everything there was interesting and different from Grandma's church. I listened intently in the Sunday School class. After the story, the teacher had a quiz. "Now if you know the Bible answer, just say it out loud," she said, smiling at us. "If you get the answer right, I will give you one of these." She held up a silver-wrapped chocolate candy. We leaned forward in our seats with anticipation.

"Who killed a giant with a sling and a stone?"

"Jesus!" I yelled. The teacher smiled at me but said nothing.

"David!" a boy beside me answered.

David? I wondered. *Who is David?*

Smiling with approval, the teacher placed a chocolate on the boy's open palm. "Good job, Benny."

"Who spent the night in the lions' den?" The teacher looked at each of us, waiting for the answer.

"Jesus," I blurted out. She quietly smiled.

"Daniel!" This time there were four or five voices shouting out the answer.

"I think you were first, Alisson." The teacher handed a blond girl a reward. But there were some mutterings of "Not fair" and "I was first."

Daniel? I thought to myself. *I've never heard of him. What about Jesus? Isn't the Bible about Jesus?* I was puzzled.

"Who was the brave queen who saved her people from being killed?" the teacher asked.

Well, that can't be Jesus, I figured. *He's not a girl.*

A girl named Jayne began bouncing in her seat and clapping her hands as she yelled out, "Esther!"

"That's right, Jayne. Good for you," the teacher said, placing one of the coveted chocolates on the table in front of Jayne.

Then the teacher looked right at me as she asked, "Who was a baby who slept in a manger?"

"Jesus?" I asked timidly.

A smile spread across her face. "That's right. It was Baby Jesus," she said, placing the delicious reward in front of me.

I managed to win three chocolate candies in the quiz that day using only Jesus as the answer, but the experience melted away as quickly as the chocolate in my mouth, leaving no lasting impression.

Though Mom had been taught the truths of the Bible by my Seventh-day Adventist grandma, she did not attend church. Her choices had led her in a different direction.

Grandma lived in a small rural town about fifteen miles from us, and I loved to spend weekends with her whenever it was my turn to do so. There was one thing I loved above all other things at Grandma's house.

I couldn't wait until Grandma would sit on the couch and begin telling me stories. Her words skillfully painted a picture of one Bible story after another. I was captivated by the stories she told me from the Bible—from the dawn of Creation, with spectacular light shining out of dense darkness, to the sound of thousands of mammals and creeping animals marching by twos and sevens up the ramp of Noah's ark. I felt like I was one of the crowd as the dazzling lightning struck the top of Mount Sinai and thunder boomed across the plain where the Israelites' tents were pitched. I listened in awe. Who was this God of might? I wanted to know Him, and God didn't ignore that desire.

One day when I was in the first grade, I arrived home to find my parents in the living room.

"Becki, come here," Dad said. "See what we've bought for you kids." He laid a book in my hands. As I turned the pages, I was elated to see pictures of the very stories my grandma had been telling me. I have no idea what caused my parents to order the ten-volume set of The Bible Story, along with a set of Uncle Arthur's Bedtime Stories, and three Tiny Tots Library books, but I was overjoyed! Would I be able to really learn about the God of the Bible through these books?

Oddly, in spite of her involvement with the spirits, that night Mom corralled us kids into the living room, where the new books were. Stroking the cover of a *The Bible Story* book, she told us, "Children, these are very special books. They are not just make-believe fantasy stories. They are *true*. They are *Bible* stories." She emphasized the words. Her reverent manner of holding the books filled us with awe. "You must be very careful with these books. You need to ask permission to use them and never handle them with unwashed hands," she said solemnly. So we washed our hands and helped her line them up in two perfect rows of beauty just beckoning for us to come and read.

That evening Mom sat down in her rocking recliner chair, and we all found a place on the floor in a semicircle at her feet while she read our first *Bedtime Story*. We listened breathlessly. The cadence in her voice brought the story to life in our young imaginations.

After that, with Mom's permission, I kept a *Bedtime Story* book in my room all the time. I pored over the illustrations and soaked up the stories like a dry sponge. It didn't take long for me to connect honesty, respectful behavior, kindness, and obedience with the Christian's God. My heart was drawn toward Him. His mercy, His love, shone through each story I read. A desire began to grow to "be good" and please Him. Unknown to me, God was revealing Himself in my heart, although the activity of the spirits remained strong in my home.

One night I woke up to hear a voice from the living room asking, "Does it really work?" My parents were gone for a couple of days, and Aunt Louise was taking care of us. Her best friend, Gabriella, was over for the weekend.

"Yeah, yeah. It really works. We do it all the time," my aunt assured her friend.

Curious to see what was happening, I got out of bed and tiptoed to watch from the doorway. In the living room there were two lighted taper candles, one at each end of the coffee table. Aunt Louise, Gabriella, and Randy were standing together.

"Of course it works," Randy repeated. "Watch this. I'll show you."

Aunt Louise was holding the Ouija board, and Randy called out in a commanding tone of voice, "Satan, if you're here, prove yourself!"

Suddenly from out of nowhere, a heavy wind blew through the front room. Both candles were extinguished as lightning flashed. Even though the windows were closed, the curtains waved and flapped.

A terrified look crossed Randy's face; Gabriella and Aunt Louise hugged each other, screaming hysterically.

In spite of the spectacle, I felt like I was in an invisible bubble, completely protected and detached from all that was happening. I had no fear.

"That's enough! We believe you!" Randy yelled above the roaring of the wind. As his terror ramped up, he yelled even louder, *"That's enough!"*

The wind quieted as quickly as it had come. The curtains once again rested in their normal position, and the two candles were lit and glowing as they had been before.

"I don't want to play that game," Gabriella said weakly. "It's too scary. I've seen enough." She wiped the tears from her eyes as she spoke.

I quietly closed my bedroom door and went back to bed. *You guys should've known better*, I thought with a touch of disgust. *You could have been hurt.* It was respect for this unseen power that would lead me to make a significant decision one day.

3

Truth or Fiction?

My hands were submerged in the bubbles of the dishwater. As I wiped the plates with a sponge and mechanically rinsed them and placed them in the dish rack, my mind was far away. Gazing into the backyard, I envisioned a swimming pool. The water was sparkling in the summer sun. There were outbursts from my friends as I imagined them tossing a ball from one to the other in a rousing game of keep-away.

Oh to have a pool in that big backyard! It was a perfectly logical idea for an eleven-year-old. Swimming was one of my favorite summer activities. Why not have a pool big enough for all of my friends too? I had just finished the dishes as my dad walked into the kitchen.

"Dad," I said, my heart thumping expectantly. "I have a great idea!"

"Uh-huh," he replied. "An idea?"

"Yes," I said with optimism. "I was looking at our backyard . . ."

"Uh-huh." He looked out the window.

"And you know, it looks just right . . ."

"For what?" He turned to me.

I continued, "Just right for a pool." I waited for his response.

"Sure, honey," he said to my delight. "We can go buy a little wading pool for you and the kids."

"Da-a-a-a-d-d," I groaned. "Not a wading pool. A *real* pool. You know, with cement, filters—twelve feet in the deep end!" And then I said it, the crowning feature of my dream pool: "With a dippity-do slide." I held my breath.

It took a moment for him to actually comprehend what I was talking about. But his reply was decided.

"Oh, no, Becki. We don't have money to build a pool like that." He shook his head. "That's for rich folks."

His tone was so final, I didn't have the gumption even to beg. With slumping shoulders, I turned and walked down the hall to my room. But it was hard to let go of that dream. It was such a *good* one. Surely there was some way I could get a pool into our backyard.

And that's when it occurred to me. Why hadn't I thought of it before? In all the world, I knew of two sources of power: God and Satan.

From what I'd read in the *Bedtime Stories*, God could save children lost in a storm, recover a lost quarter, turn enemies into friends, send food to orphans—all in answer to their prayers. It was impressive. Yes, God could perform amazing things, according to the stories I was reading.

But Mom never talks with God, and He's not my God either. That left only Satan. I had *seen* his power.

Thoughtfully I weighed the choices. Whom should I ask to grant my wish? As I pictured asking God for a pool, I imagined Him drawing back in shock and asking, "Why should I answer your prayer? I don't know you."

I had to admit, He would have every right to ask me that. With the almost daily Ouija board sessions, the occasional weekend parties, and the regular presence of spirits who made themselves visible, I had little right to ask God for anything. I was not one of His people.

That sealed my decision, and I got right down to business.

Kneeling beside my bed, I prayed, "Satan, I really want that swimming pool. If you get it for me, then I'll be yours. Thank you. Amen."

As I got up from my knees, I couldn't help asking myself, *I wonder what Jesus thought of my prayer?* As if in answer, I instantly saw His face appear on the wall across from me. He was crying, and it looked like I had hurt His feelings. Then the picture vanished.

Stunned, I sat on my bed. *Why would Jesus be hurt by me praying to Satan?* I wondered. At this point in my life, I had no concept of how much God loved me. I had no idea that He was interested in me and wanted me to come to Him with all of my desires.

For several weeks I checked the mailbox daily, waiting for

the notice that I had won the prize money that would build my dream pool. I finally had to admit that my deal with the devil was no good. Although he didn't deliver on his end, I was to find out how seriously he took my side of the deal—to "be his."

This might seem strange, but many times I could sense the presence of unseen beings. I was being watched, and I knew it. Thankfully, it wasn't just Satan who was watching me. Though I didn't know it then, there was One whose purpose was "to seek and to save that which was lost" (Luke 19:10).

One day after finishing my homework, I opened one of our *Bible Story* books. I had finished the *Bedtime Stories* and had recently started to read the *Bible Story* library. I was in the habit of doing my homework first and then treating myself to a chapter in the *Bible Story* books.

On this particular night, I read about a young boy who used a stone in a slingshot to kill a giant. The drama of the scene captured my imagination. At the chapter's end, I closed the book and sat on my bed, reliving the exciting tale—the booming voice of Goliath threatening the boy from across the valley; the trembling soldiers of Israel; the courageous words of the youth as he ran forward to meet the giant; the single stone slung from the boy's sling overcoming the giant and his whole army. It seemed incredible. *Are these stories really true?* I thought. As a child, I had not questioned the fantastic tales when Grandma had told them. But now I wondered at the amazing events. I looked at the blue book in my lap. It seemed that if I only knew that this story *really* was in the Bible, I could know it was true. But without a Bible, I had no idea.

A seed of longing was planted at that moment. *Wouldn't it be something if I could have a Bible of my own?* I thought.

I was thirteen years old when our family went to visit my mom's brother and sister-in-law. They lived right down the street from Grandma. When we got out of the car, Randy must have been wanting one of Grandma's chocolate chip cookies. "Hey, Mom," he said. "Becki and I are going down to see Grandma."

"OK," Mom said, "but we'll be having dinner soon."

So off we went. Randy tapped on Grandma's door when we got there, and we heard her call out, "Come in!"

Walking into her living room, we were surprised to see a well-dressed man stand to his feet. Grandma's face broke into a smile when she saw us.

"How good to see you!" she exclaimed. We went to give her a hug. "These are my grandchildren," she said to the visitor. Then to us she said, "I want you to meet the pastor of my church—Pastor John."

He extended his hand to each of us.

"We were reading the Bible," Grandma said. Sure enough, she had a Bible lying on the arm of her overstuffed chair.

"That's really cool, Grandma," I said.

Sensing my interest, the pastor asked, "Do you guys have Bibles?"

"No." We both shook our heads.

"Well, you're old enough to have a Bible," the pastor said. "Would you like one?"

Really? I thought. *Aren't Bibles just for old people—like Grandma?*

"Sure, I'd like to have a Bible," Randy said.

"Yeah, me too," I chimed in, excited about the possibility of having a Bible of my own.

"I happen to have some Bibles in my car. Wait right here and I'll get you one."

He probably has some old Bibles no one else wants, I thought skeptically. But when he returned, he was holding two brand-new Bibles still wrapped in cellophane. I saw the words *Holy Bible* in large print on the covers.

After unwrapping the Bibles, Pastor John wrote something inside the cover of each one. Then he showed us the maps and the dictionaries in the back of the Bibles.

Wow, a brand-new Holy Bible, I thought excitedly. Grandma had said that God is holy. *So the Bible is holy like God,* I reasoned.

"Maybe you'd like to have these Bible lessons too." Pastor John held up a set of lessons. "These are studies on different topics, such as, *Can the Bible Be Trusted?*" he said as I looked at the colorful illustrations.

When we returned home, Randy placed the whole set of Amazing Facts Bible study guides on the coffee table in our front room and then promptly went outside to play football. I carefully arranged the lessons like a fan, hoping others in the family would be attracted to them.

Once in my room, I sat on my bed, holding my Bible. *So this Bible is either true or false,* I thought. *It can't be a mixture of truth splattered with fiction. It's either truth all the way or it's fiction all the way. If it's true, I might want to pay attention. If I reject it, then the consequences could be serious. If it's false, then anything goes. I can live for myself without any concern for anyone else, because if the Bible isn't true, then there's no God or heaven and there's no devil or hell.* It seemed clear to me that the first thing I needed to do was figure out whether the Bible taught the truth. I wasn't exactly sure how I would do that, but I fully intended to keep my antenna up and be on the alert until I figured it out.

I opened my Bible with a mixture of excitement, curiosity, and awe. My eagerness was as if I was looking over a bakery case of delectable pastries, trying to decide what to have first.

There were colored maps and a concordance in the back. Then I searched for the red print that Pastor John had said were Jesus' own words. Bringing the Bible up close to my face, I enjoyed the fragrance of its pages. Within the front cover I noticed some handwriting in red pen. Pastor John had written my name and the date.

Going back to where the red words were, I began reading. I was focused on one thing: *Who was Jesus?*

4

Experiences or the Bible?

Days went by, and no one else in the family picked up the Amazing Facts Bible lessons, so I gathered them and took them to my bedroom. I didn't want them to be thrown out like the weekly newspaper.

The first lesson I decided to read was "The Celestial City in Space." I had always figured there was a heaven. Now when I read from the Bible all that God had planned, I actually thought I'd like to go. Another day, when I picked out the lesson titled "Are the Dead Really Dead?" I chuckled.

"That's easy," I said out loud. "I already know the answer to this question before even looking in the Bible!" I began reading the Bible texts that were in the lesson.

> His spirit departs, he returns to his earth;

In that very day his plans perish (Psalm 146:4).

For the living know that they will die;
But the dead know nothing,
And they have no more reward,
For the memory of them is forgotten (Ecclesiastes 9:5).

That can't be right, I concluded. The writer of these lessons obviously didn't know what I knew. Why, Mom talked with spirits of the dead using the Ouija game all the time! *If the dead know nothing, then who is my mom talking to?* The spirits were "in the know" regarding the past and the present. They also knew a great deal about the future and shared it with my mom regularly.

But when I got to the Bible verse that stated, "For they are spirits of demons, performing signs, which go out to the kings of the earth and of the whole world, to gather them to the battle of that great day of God Almighty" (Revelation 16:14), I was alarmed. The idea that the spirits I saw in our home were devils had never occurred to me. Devils were evil.

After slipping into bed that night, I tried to figure it out. When Mom had contact with the spirits, I thought they were the souls of the dead or maybe they were angels from heaven. But after reading the verses in the Holy Bible that said the dead were *not* roaming around but in the grave, I was confused. What should I believe: My experiences with the supernatural or the Bible's explanation? What's more, to think that these spirits were devils shook me deeply. Who were the spirits that were in my home?

Experiences or the Bible? | 35

This was still on my mind when I came home from basketball practice one afternoon and found my brother, sister, and their friends gathered around Mom in her recliner with the Ouija board on her lap.

As I passed them on my way to my room, DJ called after me, "Hey, Becki, do you have any questions you want to ask Ouija?"

I had not been joining them in this activity, so they were not surprised when I replied, "Nah." But suddenly I remembered something that had been troubling me since I'd read that Bible study on death. I stopped abruptly and turned around.

"Yes, I do have a question," I said, walking over to the group. They waited expectantly. Mom had her right hand resting on the message indicator as usual, and I asked, "Are you a good spirit?"

Immediately the message indicator dashed up to the word *yes* in the upper left corner of the board.

DJ said, "OK, it's a good spirit." He was speaking more to the others than to me. Everyone looked at me with wondering eyes, waiting for my next question.

"Do you know who Jesus is?" I asked. Everyone watched the message indicator with interest as it slid up to the word in the corner.

"Yes," chorused DJ and the others while the message indicator moved back to the center of the board.

"Were you at the cross when He was crucified?" I asked. Again the message indicator glided over the board to the word *yes*.

Now I asked the question I believed would tell me if these

spirits were good spirits from heaven or devils as my Bible said. "Were you sad to see Jesus on the cross?" All eyes watched the message indicator dash up to the word *no*, then back to the center of the board.

DJ started laughing and shaking his head in disbelief. "It's lying," he said, looking toward me. "It can't be a good spirit." The message indicator raced up to the word *yes*. DJ laughed again.

Rewording my question to make sure there was no misunderstanding, I asked, "Were you happy to see Jesus on the cross?"

Immediately the indicator raced up to the word *yes*.

DJ laughed harder. "You're a *good* spirit?" he asked.

The message indicator slid up to the word *yes*.

"Then you were *sorry* to see Jesus on the cross," DJ said confidently.

The message indicator slid up to the word *no*.

DJ shook his head in disbelief. "You're *lying*," he repeated emphatically. The message indicator moved up to the word *no*.

Glancing at DJ, Mom said, "You guys better stop. They're getting angry."

DJ laughed. "Yeah, because they're lying." Then, addressing the spirit, he said, "You can't be a *good* spirit and at the same time happy to see Jesus on the cross."

"Becki, do you have any other questions you'd like to ask?" Mom asked. I sensed she was hoping I'd change the subject.

"No," I said. "I've seen enough." I turned and headed for my bedroom while they continued the game.

Now I was concerned. Before, I had not understood the spirits to be enemies of Jesus. Though I had not seen the truth before about Satan's use of the Ouija game, God allowed me to see that they were lying, deceptive spirits full of complete hatred of Jesus.

If the Bible was telling the truth, then that meant the old man who had disappeared in my bedroom was really a devil or an evil spirit. The spirit I saw who poured out my Aunt Ciara's coffee was a spirit of Satan's. Was it possible that my mother was playing a game empowered by demons, and she did it *knowingly*?

This question had not been resolved the night Cindy came to my friend's house and called me to come home. That was the night I found my mother in a trance—the night of the showdown with supernatural powers.

As we all stood around the table looking at Mom, Debbie's plea hung in the air: "Becki, *do* something!"

My family had come to regard me as the "religious one." Though I had not advertised my reading of The Bible Story or the Bedtime stories books, it had been noted that I was the one interested in them. Now with Mom's playmate, the Ouija board, acting more like an enemy, they wanted me to rescue her.

It wasn't that I was afraid of a fight. I had been known to break older kids' noses in street fights. But how should one fight a spirit? How could I help Mom?

Randy had an idea. "Becki, where is your Bible?" he asked.

"In my room," I answered.

He ran to my room and got it. Laying it on the Ouija board, he opened it and began to read: "In the beginning God created the heavens and the earth. The earth was without form, and void; and darkness was on the face of the deep. And the Spirit of God was hovering over the face of the waters" (Genesis 1:1, 2). His voice had the ring of authority.

He had placed the Bible on the Ouija board below the message indictor. Now it began to ram itself against the Bible. The message indicator appeared to be trying to knock the Bible off the board, but Randy steadied it with his hands.

He continued to read, "Then God said, 'Let there be light'" (Genesis 1:3). I could hear Debbie whimpering in her chair. Mom's statue-like appearance remained unchanged.

Suddenly the message indicator rose up into the air by itself and dove at Randy. He slapped it away and continued to read. Whizzing through the air, the indicator headed for Mom's forehead, but passed above her and flew off toward the cookstove. There it spun around and came back to Randy, trying to hit him again. Marking his place in the Bible with his finger, he slapped it down. It dropped onto the board and began ramming itself against the Bible again. Then pointing at the word *no*, the indicator smashed hard into the Bible, but Randy held it in place. Finally, it slid off the board onto the floor beside Mom's chair. It moved behind her, spinning wildly like a top, until it finally slowed and then stopped.

"It died," DJ declared solemnly.

Mom gasped for breath. Her eyes made an effort to come into focus, and she looked confused.

DJ put his face down close to hers and tapped her shoulder lightly. "Do you know who I am?" he asked.

"DJ," she said.

Then he held up his fingers. "How many fingers do you see, Mom?"

Hesitating, she looked around at us. "Three." We nodded at one another.

DJ turned to Randy and said, "You can stop reading the Bible now. We have our Mom back, and she's OK."

Mom still looked dazed, however. She seemed to have no idea what had taken place.

"I was playing the game as usual," she said, "when the spirit began insisting, 'Let me in. I want your body.'" Mom's eyes were wide as she recalled what happened. "Of course, I resisted the suggestion, but they overpowered me—they just took over."

Debbie was wiping her eyes with relief. "That's not funny. I swear I'll *never* play that game again!" Still processing the shock, everyone wandered into the living room.

Standing alone in the kitchen looking at the open Bible still resting on the Ouija board, I pondered what had just taken place. I had just witnessed the power of the Bible overcome the spirit working the Ouija board game.

My mind recalled the words of Revelation 16:14: "For they are spirits of demons, performing signs, which go out to the kings of the earth and of the whole world, to gather them to the battle of that great day of God Almighty." If the devils were against God in "that great day," then Satan and God were enemies! It was as if a spotlight was shining on that fact.

I took my Bible off the Ouija board and went to my room.

For me, this spectacle had unveiled the spirits' deceptive game. For the first time, I saw clearly that the spirits of the Ouija game and Satan were on the side of evil and that the Power behind the Bible had protected Mom—maybe saving her life!

Now at a crossroads, I made a decision: *I'm going to believe my Bible.* That night, after the dramatic demonstration of the spirits' hatred for the God of the Bible, I felt a need for protection. Wrapping my arms around my Bible as a child would cuddle her favorite teddy bear, I drifted off to sleep. After this, I was never without my Bible at bedtime.

5

Discoveries

One afternoon a few weeks later, Randy, Cindy, DJ, and I were sprawled out on the living room floor watching TV. Mom was at the table with her Ouija board. I heard her sigh several times in frustration. Suddenly she jumped to her feet.

"They won't talk to me," she complained, referring to the spirits as she brushed by us on her way to her bedroom. "They're angry, because you guys put the Bible on the Ouija board. They *hate* the Bible!" No one said anything, but we knew she was furious.

Odd magazines containing life-after-death experiences began showing up on our coffee table. In addition, two ladies came at different times. One taught Mom how to read palms and coffee cups; the other one taught her to read tarot cards.

While I didn't know much about these occultic practices, I sensed they were in the same category as the Ouija board. Mom must have figured that if the spirits weren't going to talk with her through the Ouija board, then she'd use other methods to communicate with them.

One day the mailman delivered four large, heavy boxes. "Hey, there's a box for each of us," Randy said, looking at DJ, Cindy, and me. "Let's see what's inside!"

Driven by curiosity, we each began tearing open the boxes. They were all full of books.

"Maybe these books are like those *Bible Story* books," I said hopefully.

"Yeah," Randy agreed, slitting the tape with his knife. "Let's get a look." He pulled out a book and handed it to Cindy. DJ and I grabbed one from our boxes and started flipping through the pages.

I don't know what the others were seeing, because no one said anything as the pages turned. But I know what *I* saw—graphic pictures of human sacrifices of young boys and girls as well as men and women. Animals being sacrificed were pictured, as well as voodoo dolls with needles poked into them. One page had a "magic" wand and pictures showing how to make it, hold it, and use it.

Peering up from the book I was looking at, I saw Randy and DJ gawking at their books. They appeared to be as dumbfounded as I was. Suddenly Randy yanked Cindy's book away from her.

"Hey!" she yelled. "Why'd you do that?"

"These aren't like the *Bible Story* books," he told her. "I don't think we should be reading them." In silent agreement we closed the books, put them back into the boxes, and went outside.

Weeks and even months went by. Every now and then Mom would get out the Ouija game to play with it, but the spirits still refused to talk with her.

One afternoon Mom erupted from her bedroom. "I can't get that Ouija board to work!" she yelled at me. "The spirits are angry, because you guys put the Bible on top of it." Jabbing her finger at me, she yelled, "Becki, did you know the spirits hate the Bible? They *hate* it!" She stormed into the kitchen and began to fix dinner. *Why do you want to play with such a deadly game anyway?* I wondered. *You should get rid of it.*

Coming into the living room after basketball practice one day, I found Mom and Randy sitting on the couch and having an intense conversation. "Hey, Becki," Randy called out to me, "we were just talking about maybe starting a club dedicated to the worship of Satan. I think I could get Derrick, Jay, and Marcus to join." He looked at Mom. "How about some of your friends?" She named a few. Then he turned to me and asked, "Are you interested in joining us?"

I didn't need to think very long about that. I had been doing a lot of thinking lately. "No, I don't want to be involved," I said. They accepted my response without further comment.

It seemed that I was moving away from the spirits and closer to the Bible the more time I spent reading it, while Mom, with her interest in the occultic encyclopedias, was moving toward the spirits and away from God.

One day when I came home from school, DJ greeted me with a strange look on his face. "Look, Becki," he said, pointing to his right. I looked and saw Mom on the floor on her hands and knees in the middle of a circle made of toilet paper. It appeared that she had fashioned an emblem patterned after something from her occultic encyclopedias.

"Watch," DJ said. He stepped closer to the circle and placed his foot on the toilet paper as if he were going to enter the circle. Mom lunged toward him and began slapping at his legs to keep him out. She was making weird beastly sounds as if she were an angry, growling dog protecting its territory. A wild look flashed in her eyes.

DJ stepped away and moved toward another part of the circle, once again stepping onto the toilet paper as if he were going to enter the circle. Mom whirled on her knees and made angry snarling growls, slapping at DJ's legs to keep him out.

He looked at me and asked, "What do you think of that?"

I shrugged my shoulders. "I don't know." It was Mom's body I was seeing, but something else was inside of her.

Mystified, DJ and I stood there watching our mom crawling around in the circle with a crazy look in her eyes, making strange beastly sounds. After a few minutes she lay down and appeared to fall asleep. About thirty seconds later she "woke up." Sitting up, she suddenly grabbed all the toilet paper together and threw it away in the bathroom. Then she came back into the front room where we were and sat down to read as if nothing peculiar had happened. DJ and I looked at each other and shrugged. I don't know what he was thinking, but I wondered, *Could a demon really inhabit a human body?*

About this time, I thought it would be a good idea to read the Bible through from start to finish. As I was making my way through the Old Testament books, I came across this statement: "Speak to the children of Israel, saying, 'These are the animals which you may eat among all the animals that are on the earth'" (Leviticus 11:2). I sat up from my lounging position on the bed and read the whole chapter over again. Here, in the eleventh chapter of Leviticus, God was listing the animals that Israel was to eat and not eat. God designated which animals were "clean" and all right to eat and which were "unclean." I was fascinated. It had never occurred to me that God cared about what I ate.

I had eaten several of the "unclean" birds and sea creatures as well as the "unclean" land animals. But the truth was that I didn't like meat. Mom used to have to set the timer on me at mealtimes. "Becki, you have ten minutes to eat your meat, or you're going to get a spanking," she'd say. I had received a few spankings over the years for this indiscretion. One day Mom had even taken a picture of me sleeping at the dining table with my meat still on my dinner plate in front of me. I wasn't trying to be stubborn or rebellious; I just didn't care for meat.

Wandering into the kitchen where Mom was, I immediately smelled them. Mom was cooking pork chops for supper. Still holding my Bible, I asked, "Hey, Mom, did you know the Bible says we're not supposed to eat pigs?"

"Oh, yeah, I know that," she answered as matter-of-factly

as if I'd told her that Washington, DC, is the capitol of the United States. She flipped the pork chops as the grease splattered in the frying pan.

"Well, if I don't want to eat it, do I have to?" I held my breath waiting for her answer.

She paused a moment, thinking. "I guess not, if you don't want to."

I was so excited, I decided to push my good fortune just a bit further. "If I don't want to eat *any* meat, do I have to?" I stood motionless beside her while she thought.

"I suppose if you don't want to eat any meat," she said slowly, "then you can eat peanut butter and get your protein that way." She smiled and continued with her cooking.

"OK. Thanks, Mom." I tried to sound calm, but inside I was overjoyed. That was great! *Now I don't have to eat any meat at all.* I wasted no time exercising my new freedom in diet. That night, while the rest of the family ate pork chops, I slathered a piece of bread with chunky peanut butter and relished every bite—much to the amazement of my watching brothers and sister. Their questioning looks seemed to say, "Peanut butter over meat—*really*?"

Mom didn't discourage me from reading and following the Bible, but it was becoming apparent that she didn't accept God's Word as her authority. It seemed to me there had been some red flags that should have warned her she was following the wrong leader. But instead, her continued interest in the occult led to a horrific happening one night.

Cindy and I were asleep in our bedroom. Suddenly a loud

crash awakened me. The bedroom door had been thrown open with such force it was bouncing back on its hinges. *That's what woke me up*, I thought. As my eyes adjusted to the darkness, what I saw coming through the door forced me to full alert. I broke into a cold sweat.

6

Night Attack

My mother was barely recognizable as she came into the room on her hands and knees. It was immediately evident to me that she was under the full control of a demon. Possessed.

Her eyes radiated a brownish, brick-red color. From somewhere deep in her body came low, ghastly, beast-like groans and mutterings. She was jerking and twisting in ways I'd never seen a human body move. At times her head twisted with such violent force it seemed as if would snap off.

"I hate you!" The demon's deep, gravelly voice was accompanied by the sound of rolling ocean waves. More like a beast than a human, it repeated with greater emphasis, "I *hate* you!" My heart raced as the demonic, glowing eyes focused on me.

"I'm going to kill you." The words chilled me to the bone. "*I hate you.*"

Cindy, wake up! I screamed in silence. *How can she sleep through this?* But she slumbered on, unaware of the ordeal happening on the lower bunk.

Mom's invaded body continued to crawl toward me. I opened my mouth trying to scream, but I had no voice. I attempted to bolt from my bed, but I was frozen with fear, and my heart drummed in my ears.

That's when I felt it. I was holding my Bible. Instinctively I had reached for it when I was jolted awake and was now holding it tightly against my chest.

"Becki, you have your Bible. Pray!" a voice rang in my head.

I only knew two prayers. The rhyming rhythm of the most common one jingled through my thoughts:

Thank you for the world so sweet,
Thank you for the food we eat,
Thank you for the birds that sing,
Thank you, God, for ev'rything.[1]

Somehow this prepackaged prayer felt dismally inadequate—about as effective as waving a willow twig in the face of a charging grizzly bear. The demon's beastly form had progressed to the head of my bed. I clung in desperation to my Bible, hoping for help and protection.

"Becki, you have your Bible. Pray!" the voice urged again.

Doubts overwhelmed my mind. *Why would God listen to me?*

I'm not a Christian. A cold wave passed over me as I faced the awful truth—He was not *my* God. The stark admission of this truth inside my mind matched the terror happening outside of me. Yet in the midst of this turmoil the voice urged, *Pray, Becki, pray!*

The unearthly creature was beside me now—an ambiance of pulsating hate and anger. In a reflex of fear, I raced through the words of the bedtime prayer:

Now I lay me down to sleep,
I pray the Lord my soul to keep,
If I should die before I wake . . .

That is exactly where I was—at death's door. Mom's hands were lifted off the floor and placed purposefully on the edge of my bed. Gripping my Bible and staring into the demon's angry eyes, I began to shake uncontrollably.

This moment of confrontation pulled from me my first original prayer. It was simple and right to the point. *Help! Jesus. Please help me! I'm going to die!*

A troubling thought inserted itself into my trauma. *Do you believe that God is real? There's no point in praying to God if you don't believe that He's real. Do you believe?*

Experiences with the spirits flashed through my mind. I had seen that Satan was real. *Was God as real as Satan?*

With the calculation of a stalking cat ready to spring, Mom's hands slowly lifted off my bed. *I am about to die at the hands of my own mother*, I realized. Convinced of my fate, I lunged toward God like a drowning swimmer exerting her final effort for the lifesaving buoy. Silently I prayed, *Jesus please help me. You have to be real! You have to be* real*! I'm going to die!*

With lightning speed, an angel flashed to my side seemingly from nowhere. His left arm was extended around my back, and his white-robed right arm made a sharp downward motion about eight inches in front of my face. He then placed his right arm around me. I was literally wrapped in the arms of a shimmering angel.

The hands of my demon-possessed mom stopped a short distance from my throat and pulled back. Throwing the angel a defiant look, the evil spirit inside my mom let out a deep, terrifying growl, snapping her head sharply.

Glowing with a living radiance, the angel remained unintimidated and calm. The demon and the angel exchanged looks as if they knew each other, but neither spoke a word. The angel's nonverbal expression seemed to say, "Go ahead and try what you like, but you're not going to hurt her."

Mom's hands were raised again in another attempt by the demon to choke me, but they stopped in the same place as if there was an invisible wall the demon could not penetrate.

With the second foiling of his plans, the demon's eyes narrowed. Mom's face turned a crimson red, and snarls emanated from the hunter that had been denied its victim. In a final attempt, the demon tried to press through the unseen barrier.

I watched in horror as the muscles in Mom's arms grew and began to bulge like a well-seasoned body builder. Veins began to pop out on her neck. Beads of perspiration stood out on her forehead as the spirit's desperation mounted. The demon had no intention of losing this battle. Yet Mom's hands slid down to the floor in defeat.

At that moment, Cindy stirred. As she rolled over, Mom's face turned upward, her mouth twisting into a phony, disgusting grin. Cindy promptly let out a fearful scream and rolled over, pulling the sheets over her head.

Casting a look of defiance at the angel, the demon turned to leave. Mom began crawling back toward the door. Stopping now and then, her body would jerk and the demon's low grumblings would rumble out of her. At the door, she turned and crawled into our front room.

Had the demon left her? I wanted to run and check for a pulse or breath, but I was frozen to my bed.

"It's OK, Becki. You can go back to sleep now." The angel spoke with gentle authority.

But I silently resisted. *What if the awful thing returns? How can I just lie down and go to sleep as if nothing has happened?*

Seeming to understand my fears, the angel said, "He won't come back."

Then the angel stood up. Rainbow colors glistened like diamonds and flashed in all directions from his wings. The tall, fluffy wings reminded me of the cotton batting we used at Christmas to decorate the windowsills.

Then the angel sat down on the bed facing me. He began running his fingers through my hair as a mother comforts a frightened child. "God has heard your prayer, and He sent me here to be with you." The angel's voice was soothing. "I'm going to stay right here beside you all night." For a moment my body relaxed. "The demon is not coming back. God won't let him," the angel reassured me.

I had never known such a sense of protection. In the security of this moment, as I lay back down, my attention was drawn to the angel. His skin, face, and hands had a golden sheen. Full of life, his hair was a shining silvery white, which, I imagined, was never cut, since that would be cutting away part of that life. Vibrant life emanated from his entire being.

My pulse continued to race, and my mind remained on high alert. However, in spite of my anxious fears, in time, my heart slowed to a normal rhythm, and though I'd meant to stay awake, slowly my eyes shut.

When I awoke in the morning, I found myself asleep on my stomach with my face toward the wall. My first thought was of the angel. *Was he still there as he'd promised?* I turned my head.

---

1. Anonymous, "A Child's 'Thank You,' " public domain.

7

Prayer Panic

As I began to roll over, I felt the weight of his presence lifting off the bed and caught a glimpse of the angel's form just as he disappeared through the ceiling. *He kept his promise!* My heart thrilled with that realization. Scrunching my pillow behind me, I leaned against it, holding my Bible and reviewing the events of the night.

God is real! I thought. After the experience with the Bible on top of the Ouija board I thought He *might* be real, but now I knew without any doubt—*God is real.* He had heard my unspoken prayer. And then the thought hit me like a water balloon in the face—*He listens to prayers from people who aren't even Christians!* My skin tingled with with goose bumps. *Why would He care about me?*

The contrast between Satan's demon and the angel of God

came into clearer focus. Satan is the epitome of hate and anger. God is kind, gentle, and loving. Satan's demon would have strangled me if he could have, while God's angel lovingly embraced me. Satan's demon was powerful, but God's angel was more powerful. Satan creates fear and terror; God gives comfort and peace. Satan obviously wanted me dead, but God sent an angel to save my life. *Why?* I marveled again.

Holding my Bible at arm's length, I studied it. Then laying it down on my lap, I began turning its pages. My pulse quickened. Where in this book could I find out how to become a Christian? I hoped with all my heart I could find it. But at this moment, all I knew was that I wanted Jesus—not Satan—to be my God.

The household began to stir. I heard Randy talking with Dad in the front room; but I was holding my breath, waiting for Mom's voice. When I heard her talking, I exhaled. "She's OK," I sighed. Gathering my courage, I came out of the bedroom and acted as if everything were fine.

As awful as that night had been, school assignments and activities demanded my attention. I cared about my grades, and the need to study moved me back into my routine.

But something had changed. That night I had realized that God was safe. The devil's mask had been torn away. I knew what Satan thought of me—and it was not good.

Mom had recently had back surgery. Two ladies came to the door.

"Becki," Mom said as I showed them in, "this is Mrs. Denise Dollmeyer, the head nurse of the hospital where I had surgery."

From her recliner, Mom nodded toward the older woman. "She's also the wife of the Seventh-day Adventist pastor in town."

Mrs. Dollmeyer smiled warmly and said, "Hello." Then she introduced her young friend. "This is Donna. She's a member of my church." While Mrs. Dollmeyer and Mom continued with their small talk, I studied Donna. She looked to be a few years older than me. Just then Randy came out of his bedroom.

"I see you have young people who are just the right age for a youth group we're starting this summer," Mrs. Dollmeyer told Mom. Deciding he didn't want to be a part of this conversation, Randy hurried his steps and disappeared out the front door. That left me facing this unwanted attention alone. I felt like a trapped animal.

Mom broke the awkward silence. "How about it, Becki? Would you like to join their youth group?"

I broke out in a cold sweat. "I'm not really sure about that," I said as my mind fished for one excuse after another.

"Oh, but we'll have so much fun," Donna said, her eyes dancing with enthusiasm. "We're going to sing some cool songs, play games, and then talk about what Jesus means to us."

I had never heard of such a group. In spite of my reservations, the mention of singing had caught my attention. I loved music, and I couldn't help wondering, *What would kids my age have to say about Jesus? What did Jesus mean to them?*

Mrs. Dollmeyer, Donna, and Mom were now staring at me. Fear of meeting kids my own age gripped me again. "I'm not sure how I'd get there. I don't drive," I said hesitantly.

Donna quickly volunteered, "I know where you live, and I have my own car. I'll pick you up, and you can hang out with me!"

I looked at Mom half wishing she would say no. But instead she said encouragingly, "It's OK with me if you'd like to go, Becki."

Having no reasonable excuse, I conceded. "Sure, I'd like to come." However, the thought of being with a group of "saintly" Christians was a little nerve-racking.

Donna showed up on time, and when we walked into the church, the group was singing a familiar tune. It would be the *only* one I would recognize all evening. I began singing along.

Barry and Linda, a married couple, were the youth leaders. About a dozen young people sat on couches or cross-legged on the floor. Right away we were given the assignment of finding a person who was wearing our favorite color. In the mad search from person to person, I forgot how anxious I'd felt in the car on the way over.

"OK," Barry called, finally clapping his hands to get our attention. "Let's get all the chairs and couches back into a circle." *I wonder what game this will be*, I thought as I sat down.

"You know, we've already had such a great time with our friends—and even met some new friends." Barry looked at me with an accepting smile. "And when we get together, it is the perfect opportunity to talk with our best Friend of all, Jesus." He reached out and took Linda's hand. Then he reached for the hand of the guy on his right. Everyone else followed his lead.

Completely pushed out of my comfort zone, I took the hands

of the girls on either side of me. Barry continued, "Tonight, I'll start. Let's take turns praying around the circle. Just tell Jesus what you think of Him or thank Him for the sunset tonight—whatever you want to say to Him."

As everyone bowed their heads, a cold fear gripped my heart, and my hands began to sweat. I didn't know how to pray *in a group*. What was I going to say in front of strangers?

As the prayers were being said around the room, I practiced praying by silently requesting that the floor would open and swallow me. How I longed to disappear! But that didn't happen. When my turn came, I nervously mumbled something I had heard someone else say and tacked on a quick, "Amen."

I was relieved to have made it through when the girl at my side pried her hand free. Mortified, I realized I had been gripping her hand too tightly. After she shook her hand to restore the circulation, she gently took my hand again. Finally the prayer ordeal ended.

"Let's open our Bibles," Barry said.

Now this I can get into, I thought. We began reading about a woman who probably felt a lot more uncomfortable than I had felt during prayer. As the story unfolded, a woman accused of adultery was dragged into the middle of a church crowd and dumped in front of them. I winced sharply, feeling her shame.

"Does anyone identify with how this woman felt?" Barry asked.

A girl named Maria spoke up. "I remember a time I did something wrong and my teacher called me to a corner of the room to talk quietly to me." Maria stared at her hands. "She didn't—like—announce what I'd done to the world."

And that is what struck me about Jesus in the story. Though the woman was guilty, He silently convicted her accusers and encouraged the woman to stop sinning without condemning her.

When I left that night, I was impressed with the insight and Bible knowledge these kids had. I was touched by their expressions of love and trust in Jesus throughout the discussion. It was evident they actually loved Jesus and knew He loved them.

After that, sometimes the group met at someone's home for a potluck lunch and then went on a hike. Later we'd meet back at the home for more food, songs, and Bible discussions. There was an excursion to explore caves and a trip to the beach where we built different Bible stories in the sand and tried to guess each other's work of art.

I felt so accepted that I began to ask questions more freely. One day I was sharing with Donna some interesting things I was learning in my own reading of the Bible. "Except I haven't read the book about careers yet," I told her. "But I guess it is still a few more years before I need to get a job." She looked at me with questioning eyes.

"Which book is about careers, Becki?" she asked. "What are you talking about?"

"Oh, you know," I told her. "The book of Job. Wouldn't that be where we look to find out what career to have?" At that, Donna dissolved into giggles.

"Oh, I think you mean the book of Job," she said, trying

to control her mirth. "Job is a person. That book is about a man," she explained, wiping her eyes. "Job loves God. The devil believes that he can get Job to sin, and God allows the devil to try in order to prove how much Job really loves and trusts Him. Don't skip that book, Becki. I think you'll like it."

There was a lot to learn. One Sabbath after a short sermon, everyone stood up and started moving to different areas of the church. Some were going downstairs; others were moving to the main-level Sabbath School classrooms. I followed the youth group up into the balcony. Donna asked if she could "serve" me. I had no clue what she was talking about.

She explained that we were doing "Communion" and this was the part of the service where we washed each other's feet.

"I took a shower this morning," I whispered to her. "My feet aren't dirty."

She smiled. "I know, but this is the service of humility. We allow someone else to wash our feet, recognizing that others in the church are here to help us. Then we wash someone else's feet to show that we also are willing to serve others."

"That sounds strange," I blurted out, not fully understanding the symbol. But I slipped my sandals off to join in. Later I read in John 13 about Jesus setting the example of this very act. If Jesus had done it, that's all I needed to know.

After this service, I joined the congregation as they ate the unleavened bread and drank grape juice. The elders read 1 Corinthians 11:23–26 describing how Jesus had led out in this very first Lord's Supper. I felt honored to do what Jesus had done.

That summer my youth leaders, Barry and Linda, asked Mom if I could go with them to camp meeting. My mother knew all about camp meeting since she had been raised a Seventh-day Adventist. However, I was in for a new experience!

8

Not a Circus

When we arrived at the Gladstone camp meeting that summer, there were cabins and tents as well as trailers parked on the grass. What looked like small circus tents were scattered around, with a huge circus tent off to my right.

I was thrilled. *This is going to be great!* I'd never been to a circus before. I began looking around to see where they might be hiding the animals. Would they show the elephants first, or the tigers?

I had never seen so many happy, friendly people all in one place. Folks were running up to each other, giving hugs, and laughing freely. It reminded me of a large family reunion.

We followed clusters of youth to a smaller circus tent. "We'll start out here this morning, and then we'll go to the main tent this evening," Barry explained as we stepped through the entrance. I saw rows of benches for people to sit on and a bunch of hay covering the floor. I knew what that was for: we were going to feed the animals! I waited expectantly on the edge of my seat.

Before long, the room was buzzing with teens about my age, and then the show began. But instead of lions and tigers, a group of teenagers did a skit. When the main speaker was announced, I craned my neck to get a glimpse of Elder H. M. S. Richards Jr. *Oh wow! He's the guy my mom listens to on the* Voice of Prophecy *radio program on Sunday mornings.* He was tall and slender with silvery flecks in his dark hair. His topic—dating—immediately caught everyone's attention.

"You don't even want to leave the driveway on a date without offering a prayer," he advised. That made a lot of sense to me. I knew I wanted Jesus to be with me no matter who I was with or what I was doing. His message stirred me and remained in the recesses of my mind.

In the car on our way home, I finally figured it out. Camp meeting was not a circus act at all but a lot of Seventh-day Adventists coming together to listen to different sermons for a whole day and to hang out with friends in between.

Summer ended all too quickly, and I was back in school. But sometimes I looked forward to going to church on the weekends.

"Becki, you've got to come with us to the meetings Elder Evans is having." Linda's eyes were wide with enthusiasm. "And the Heritage Singers will be there. You will love their music!"

She was right. The blended harmonies of the group were something I'd never heard. The singers were all in formal attire—the men wearing black suits with white shirts and black ties and the ladies wearing long dresses in various pastel colors and long white gloves.

Even DJ and Cindy joined me for a couple of these evening meetings in the school auditorium. It was only a few blocks away. We all sat together and listened to the message, and then discussed what we'd heard as we walked back home.

From the Amazing Facts Bible guides I'd read, I had already learned about most of the subjects Elder Evans presented. But there was one subject in particular I'd never studied. He talked about baptism and what it means to be born again into a new life in the family of God.

"When you are born again, you will want to testify to your new birth by being baptized," Elder Evans said. Then he turned to the Bible passage that described Jesus' own baptism.

Elder Evans told about his personal struggle with alcoholism. As he recalled how God had helped him turn his back on that way of life once and for all, I thrilled to the words I was hearing. For the first time in my life, I felt there was hope for a sinner like me. Maybe even I could become a Christian.

This is what I want! I thought excitedly. *I want to be baptized just like Jesus was.*

At the end of the message that night, a piano began playing softly in the background as Elder Evans continued earnestly. "If you hear the Holy Spirit speaking to your heart—if you want to have your sins washed away in the waters of baptism—I invite you to come forward." His voice broke with emotion as people began to leave their seats and come forward. Shaking their hand or patting them kindly on the shoulder, Elder Evans directed them to a place to sit at the front.

I felt a pull inside me to get up and go forward. But I remained seated. One or two more people stood and walked to the front as Elder Evans continued to ask if there was anyone else who wanted Jesus to be the Lord of their life.

Is he going to wait until I come forward? I thought as my heart pounded. I desperately wanted to be up there sitting with those folks, but I knew I was a dreadful sinner. However, the urge to get to my feet became so strong, I feared I might actually get out of my seat! Putting my feet on the floor and leaning back against my seat, I pressed myself harder into its back in an effort to keep from rising. Then without warning, I found myself standing.

"Hey, what are you doing?" Cindy whispered in surprise.

"I can't help it. I've got to go forward," I admitted as I began inching down the row of our seats. I could feel her puzzlement, but it didn't matter.

Once at the front, I collapsed into a chair. I felt so filthy and dirty. *Why would Jesus accept a sinner like me?* But if He was offering, I longed for His cleansing blood to wash my sins away in baptism.

The singing that filled the room created an atmosphere of pure and holy love that seemed to transport me to the very edge of heaven. I imagined even the angels were joining their voices in the singing. My tears were unleashed and wouldn't stop. That's when I felt an arm encircle me. An elderly lady singing with the others patted my shoulder.

> All to Jesus I surrender,
> All to Him I freely give;
> I will ever love and trust Him,
> In His presence daily live.[1]

When the singing came to a worshipful hush, Elder Evans prayed, "Dear Father in heaven, thank You for all of these dear ones who have come forward. Please continue to lead in their lives. May they have the privilege of being washed in the blood of Jesus and becoming whiter than snow."

After his prayer, I thanked the woman who had patted my shoulder. She smiled and gave my arm a squeeze.

All the way home, I was caught up with the possibility of being washed clean from my sins—becoming whiter than snow. *Now Jesus is going to be the Lord of my life!* I reveled in anticipation.

But the cloud I was floating on collapsed as soon as I stepped through the front door. Raucous laughter from the dining room where my parents were playing cards with a couple of friends brought me back to earth. Everyone had their favorite beverage. The smell of cigarette smoke and whiskey hung heavily in the air.

How am I going to be a Christian in this home? The troubling problem loomed before me.

I paced the floor, trying to figure out what to do. I reasoned that God and Satan could not be roommates; they could not live together in the same house. They were worlds apart.

It had been only a matter of months since I'd been attacked by Satan's demon. I knew I was alive only because God had sent an angel to protect me. Would God continue His protection if the devil were in charge of this home?

In deep disappointment, I sank down on my bed. After much consideration, I concluded that probably the best thing for me to do was to lie low and wait until I was old enough to get out on my own. Then I could decide for myself who would be the God of my life.

About a week after my decision to go forward at the meeting, I was in Mom's bedroom making her bed when she opened the door to the pastor. As he seated himself on the couch, I heard him say, "Mrs. Greig, I want you to know that I am very impressed with Becki's faithful attendance at the meetings. I can see God is really working in her life."

Forgetting the bed-making, I stepped closer to the door and strained to hear Mom's response. I couldn't make out the words, but I could tell by the tone of her voice that his comments had irritated her.

He continued, "Mrs. Greig, when Elder Evans invited those who were interested in baptism to come forward, Becki responded."

There was no question about how Mom felt about that.

"Why, Becki is only fifteen years old!" she said indignantly. "You can't expect her to be able to make a decision like that at fifteen!"

I was embarrassed at her rudeness and remained hidden in her room, listening to their conversation. The pastor tried to convince Mom that baptism would be a good thing for me, but she didn't want to hear anything more about it. When he tried one last time to press the subject with her, I knew he was in trouble.

I heard a change in her tone of voice. When she was that angry, she had supernatural strength, and it was downright dangerous to be near her.

Fear gripped my heart as I heard her rise from her chair. The fact that she was still recovering from back surgery would not prevent her from doing him harm.

But seeing her fury, the pastor made a hasty retreat. I heard the door slam, then his steps hurry away. I sighed in disappointment at Mom's response and yet relief that he had escaped.

Pastor Dollmeyer never came to our home again.

---

1. Judson W. VanDeVenter, "I Surrender All," (1896).

9

Death Is Waiting

After Pastor Dollmeyer's hasty exit from our home, the enemy began hammering me with accusations. They went something like this: *If you're not going to be baptized until you're on your own, what is the point of going to church? Why be a hypocrite?*

Pastor Dollmeyer's recent sermon still rang in my ears.

"According to the Bible, we are all sinners. The Bible also teaches that we will all stand before the judgment bar of the Holy Father someday. At that time, as God looks down from His throne, Jesus will step in front of the repentant ones who believe in Him. 'This person loves Me and has asked Me to forgive their sins,' He will say. 'And Father, I ask that You accept My sacrifice and righteousness on their behalf.' Then the Father will smile and accept them as if they have never sinned.

They will receive the gift of eternal life in heaven."

But the sinners who didn't believe in Jesus, who had never asked Him to forgive them, would stand in front of the Father alone. Jesus could not be their defense, and the Father would see all the sins they had never confessed. They would be found guilty and sentenced to eternal death, for the Bible says, "The wages of sin is death" (Romans 6:23).

I was excited and frightened at the same time: excited about God's plan to save me—it gave me hope! But I was also frightened, because I'd never confessed my sins, and I knew I wasn't truly a Christian.

The decision to delay my baptism put me in constant fear. *What if Jesus comes now? I will not be ready.* I knew that my delay to follow Jesus left me living outside of God's will. That was terrifying for me. I could only hope that He would delay His coming in the clouds until I was baptized.

One day as I was taking out the trash, I had just put the lid on the can and was turning to go back into the house. That's when I had what I can describe only as a brief "vision." Before me, our backyard was transformed into a crowd of people sitting in a large room. They were looking up at an animated speaker on a stage. Everyone was listening with rapt attention to what the speaker was saying.

At that moment I heard a voice, and it sounded as if the speaker were standing right beside me. "Becki, this is you in the future." The scene suddenly vanished, and I saw my familiar backyard again. Although the voice had not been audible, it had been so clear and distinct that I knew it was not my imagination.

I was shaken by the suggestion that I would ever stand up in front of people to talk. Just the thought of giving a book report in the classroom made me tremble. The experience seemed too crazy to ever share, but it was powerfully real to me.

The routine of life carried me through graduation from high school. I was anxious to move out and start life on my own, but I knew I needed a job that would pay enough to support me. I knew that once I moved out, I would never move back home again.

In time, I got a job as a security officer at the Weyerhaeuser plant site. The pay and benefits were good. At the same time, my best friend from high school was hired as a nurse at the local hospital, so we found an apartment to rent together.

Immediately my thoughts turned to God. *Now I can be baptized, and Jesus can be my God*, I thought with eager anticipation. But every time I would plan to start attending church again, accusing thoughts crowded in. *You already had your opportunity, and you blew it. Your chance to take a stand for Jesus has come and gone. You should have been baptized a long time ago. It's too late now.*

I didn't recognize it at the time, but these were deceitful lies of the devil that beat me down into a state of depression. It was true—I'd had an opportunity to get baptized when I was fifteen, and that opportunity had long since passed. Maybe I should have gotten baptized in spite of my mom's objections. If that were true, I reasoned, it was also true that it was too late now. That led me to the next logical consideration: *If I'm not going to be in heaven, what is there in this world that's worth striving for?*

Immediately an answer popped into my mind. Alcohol! My dad, who appeared to make friends easily and had always responsibly supported his family, was never without it. Maybe I had been missing out on something.

So early one evening when Dad came home from work anticipating a couple of days off, I dropped the bomb.

"Hey, Dad, let's you and me go have a drink tonight." I could see the astonishment in his eyes as he processed what he'd just heard.

"I'm serious, Dad," I urged. "I want to know what it's like to get drunk. Let's do it; let's get drunk!" I chirped as happily as if I'd just suggested we go for a roller-coaster ride or out to the DQ.

Still in shock, he shrugged his shoulders. "OK."

That was that, and shortly we were in the car headed to the liquor store.

"So, what do you want?" Dad asked awkwardly as he pulled into the parking lot.

"Just get me something a girl would like," I told him, hoping for something that would taste good.

He emerged from the store with a tall bottle wrapped in a paper bag. Driving outside of town into the woods, he found his favorite hunting spot and poured us each a drink.

As I sipped on the bubbling beverage, a warm sensation slid down my throat. I crinkled my nose. *Why do people like this stuff?* I wondered. Dad began asking probing questions, and I found myself opening up to him about things I had never intended to share with my parents. Suddenly I felt afraid that my confessions could jeopardize the usual acceptance I enjoyed from my carefree dad. But instead, his response melted my heart.

"No matter what you have done in the past, or whatever you do in the future," he assured me, "I love you. And I always will love you!"

With Dad's reassurance hanging in the air, we both turned back to our drinks and drifted into our own quiet thoughts. It was then that I saw two angels outside my window, each surrounded by a glistening light. One was resting both arms across the windowsill of the car door, with his wings reaching high up behind him. His silver-golden hair relaxed in gentle waves on his shoulders. Behind him another angel was suspended about eight feet above the ground.

"You know, Becki, you've just heard how much your dad loves you." The angel motioned his hand toward Dad as he spoke. "We want you to know that God loves you even more than that."

I glanced over at my dad, who was still looking out his window, and then back down to the drink I was holding. *How can God love me when I'm intentionally trying to get drunk?* I wondered.

As if reading my thoughts, the angel reassured me, "He does."

"And He sent us here to tell you that," the angel in the air added.

"He did?" I questioned quietly.

"Yes, He did," he answered. They looked at each other,

nodding in agreement. The closest angel looked back at me and smiled. Then they both evaporated into the sky.

I studied my dad. I could tell he had no idea what had just happened. Because I'd had only a few sips of my drink, I knew I wasn't hallucinating. As it was, most of the still-sparkling drink in my cup was eventually dumped.

On the way back to my apartment, I pondered my excursion with Dad. I couldn't imagine angels getting drunk. I wondered how many people had been killed by a drunk driver. I winced. How many were in jail or prison because they were under the influence when the crime or accident happened? How many people's lives had been forever changed because of alcohol? How many were so addicted to alcohol that they were wandering the streets, still clinging to the partially filled bottle? What I'd thought might offer me the "good life" was dissolving fast. *No, I don't think being an alcoholic will make my life worthwhile*, I concluded.

I continued to ponder what purpose my life had apart from God. Then I came to a pivotal decision one day. On my way home from visiting with my grandmother, my car rounded a wide bend, and the community cemetery came into full view. In a dramatic way, it suddenly brought me face-to-face with reality.

Every person eventually gets buried in a cemetery, like garbage that ends up at the city dump. I thought of my mundane round of life: waking up, getting ready for work, putting in a full day, coming home, making dinner, washing the dishes, going to bed—then a repeat of that the next day and the next. Day after day, year after year. *Is that it?* I asked myself. Painfully I concluded, *There isn't anything in this world worth striving for except preparing for eternity.* So if heaven was not a possibility for me, what purpose did I have to keep on living?

Death is waiting. These words were constantly in my thoughts. I could die today or a hundred years from now, but—death is waiting.

Now I began to explore forbidden alternatives. *Well, if I'm going to die anyway,* I thought, *and there's no future after that, why prolong the inevitable?*

After considering my options, I settled on what I thought was a foolproof plan. I would sneak one of Dad's hunting rifles out of his house. All it would take was a trip into the woods and this hopelessness would be over.

All I needed was the perfect moment.

10

Divine Encounter

Arriving back at my apartment door, I fumbled with the key. Weary from my night shift and now in a depressed state of mind, I sank onto the couch. Methodically, I began to go over the details of how I would get Dad's gun.

I didn't sense the presence of someone else in the room until I heard his voice. It was an angel.

"Becki, if you don't stop right now and find something else to do, *you really will be dead!*" With that sudden realization, I knew I actually *did* want to live, and I wanted to be a Christian with all my heart. But I didn't know how. Those hopeless, haunting words rang again in my ears: *It's too late.*

Like a fast-paced movie coming to a slow-motion scene, my mind balked: *Is it really too late?*

It might have been the angel's voice reassuring me that someone cared, but whatever it was, I slowly began to gather threads of courage. The determination to end my life faded as hope glimmered. *If there really is still hope for me*, I realized, *God will have to help me know how to become a Christian.*

Pushing myself up from the couch, I went to my room. Music would create a better mood, so I switched on the radio dial. But instead of music, I heard a man's voice asking, "If Jesus were to come today—*right now*—would you be ready?"

Are you kidding me? I stared at the radio. *That's the last thing I want to hear.* I switched off the radio. In a panic now, my mind began to whirl with questions. *What would I do if Jesus did come today? Where would I run? Where would I hide? I'm not ready!*

Anger began to rise along with terror. *This is all my fault. What was I so afraid of? Why hadn't I stood up for myself and been baptized in spite of Mom's opposition?* I longed for the days when I had read my Bible and hung out with my friends at church. The tragic truth was that those days were in the past.

I shut my eyes. Bitter tears slid down my cheeks as I wished desperately for the impossible—for one more chance.

In answer to my heartfelt desire, I was pulled into a wide-awake dream. I was no longer in my bedroom listening to the wind driving the rain against my window. I was standing in a warm, sunny field of beautiful green grass as soft as a baby's blanket. Sheep were grazing around me, and baby lambs innocently frolicked together.

I was so fascinated with the grass. *Who has ever seen perfect grass like this?* I marveled. I began searching to find some weeds.

Focused as I was on the grass, I unexpectedly came upon the feet of a man. Raising my eyes, I saw a shepherd cradling a tiny lamb. *Oh, this must be the shepherd of all these sheep*, I reasoned.

When the shepherd set the lamb down and stretched out His arms for me to come to Him, I saw them—the scars in both palms. I gasped. *He's not just any shepherd*, I thought in awe. *This is Jesus!*

I chastised myself with stinging words: *Those scars are there because of your sins. You did that to Him.* It all came back to me in living color. The times when I knew I wasn't doing right, the poor choices I'd made, and the unkind words I'd said. Oh, how I wished I hadn't acted that way or said those words. But with overwhelming regret, those familiar words taunted me again: *It's too late.*

Now I noticed someone striding confidently across the field toward me. With his dark good looks and the shimmering silver threads of his sky-blue suit, he looked like the corporate executive of the world. It was not hard to guess who he was. It was Satan.

Smiling, he stepped beside me and put one arm around my shoulder as a friend would do when greeting another. He looked over at Jesus, then back at me, and spoke ever so kindly. "You don't *have* to look at Him. Just look away."

Obediently I dropped my eyes to avoid looking at Jesus' hands. My gaze rested on His feet. His sandal straps were arranged in such a way that I now saw the ugly scars etched on His feet.

Look at those scars. Your sins put those scars there. My eyes began to fill with tears. *If only I could live my life over! How different it would be.*

Satan slipped his arm off my shoulder and backed up a couple paces. His dark eyes now flashed with anger, and the kindness in his voice was gone.

"Look away," he said through clenched teeth. "You don't have to look at Him." Finally, with no attempt to hide his real feelings, he commanded, *"Look away!"*

In my desperation something snapped, and I reacted.

"What am I supposed to do? If I look down, there are His feet! If I look to the left or right, I see His hands!" I argued. Suddenly I found myself pushing against this authority that had bullied me all these years. This was truly a crossroads. I knew I had two choices: I could look up at the face of Jesus or I could look away from Him. Though I felt completely unworthy, I wanted Him so much. I chose to lift my gaze to Jesus.

I had always imagined God would be angry with me—ready to strike me out of existence because of my sins. But instead His look of incredible love captivated me. Although I was sure He was aware of every sin I'd committed my entire life, I saw in Him nothing but understanding love and acceptance.

"Won't you come to Me?" His arms opened wider. I desperately wanted to be with Him. But I hesitated, not able to believe His love was for me. "You don't want me. I'm no good. Why don't you go to those other homes over there?" I motioned to the collection of apartments nearby. "I'm sure you'll find someone much better than me there." My voice faltered.

His eyes filled with tears at my words. They ran down His

cheeks, and it was clear that I'd hurt Him. I saw a sadness in His face that I couldn't begin to comprehend.

"But I love *you*! I died for *you*!" He leaned toward me. "I can help you, take care of you, and make you happy. Won't you *let* me?" He pleaded.

"Jesus, I want to," I admitted. "I want to come to You, but I don't know *how*."

"Then turn your radio back on," He said softly, "and I will tell you how." With that He faded from my sight, and the dream ended. I was back in my room again.

Dazed, I looked around. W*as that real, or did I make it up?* There was only one way to know. *If it's nothing more than a crazy dream, I'll probably get a toothpaste commercial or the latest weather report*, I reasoned.

My hand was shaking as I reached out to turn on the radio. *Oh, please be real. Please be real, so I can find out how to come to Jesus.* Slowly I sat down on the edge of my bed to listen.

Immediately I recognized the same voice that had earlier asked, "If Jesus were to come today, would you be ready?" This time as the man spoke, I leaned forward. *That's the* Voice of Prophecy *program*, I realized. Elder H. M. S. Richards Jr. was speaking.

"No matter how much of a sinner you may think you are, no matter how far down in the depths of sin you may have sunk, *God loves you*."

My heart was racing as I stared at the radio. Was this man speaking just to me? How did he know that I was so deep in sin's mud I was about to sink?

He continued, "It is written in the book of First John, chapter one, verse nine, that 'if we confess our sins, He is faithful and just to forgive us our sins and to cleanse us from all unrighteousness.'"

That's it! I was breathless with joy. *Could it really be that simple?*

My mind was quickly filling with sins I needed to confess. Turning off the radio, I knelt by my bed. I hesitated a moment, wondering how to begin. *Maybe I'll talk to Him as if He were standing in front of me—just as He was in my dream.*

"Jesus," I began, "I know I've done this all wrong, and I'm sorry. Would You forgive me?" I was very specific about the sins I was confessing. But after mentioning three or four sins, I stopped.

I had just turned twenty years old. That was a lot of years of sins to confess. *How am I going to remember all those sins?* It was overwhelming.

In a heartbeat I found myself kneeling again in that soft, green, grassy field with Jesus standing in front of me in my wide-awake dream. I also heard laughter—hysterical, mocking laughter. Turning, I saw Satan in that shimmering, sky-blue suit laughing at my confessions with exaggerated hilarity. Then his laughing stopped abruptly, and he said with a smirk, "You can't remember your sins." At that he threw back his head and went into another fit of laughter. Finally recovering, he sneered, "If you don't remember your sins, you can't confess them, and if you don't confess them, you can't be forgiven." I felt myself wilting under the heat of his harassment as he continued his rant. "He can't have you. You are *mine.* You prayed to *me*! You asked *me* to be your god. Now you belong to *me,* and I will never let you go!"

The memory of my prayer to Satan at eleven years of age snapped me to attention.

"That's right, Satan!" I exploded indignantly. "I did pray to you. But where is the swimming pool I asked for? I've never received anything I've wanted in life from you. As a matter of fact, I've come to the place that I don't even want to live anymore. Is this all you have to offer me? Death? Why don't you just shut up and let me make up my own mind?" No sooner had I said those words than I realized my foolish boldness. *What have I done?* I thought with instant regret as I watched Satan, with hateful resolve, slowly pull back his hand, which was clenched in a tight fist. I braced myself for his powerful punch.

Catching Satan's eye, Jesus nodded His head as if to say, "Back off and let her choose."

Grudgingly Satan turned and walked away. I watched as angels came out from behind the nearby trees where they appeared to have been listening the whole time. Their eyes narrowed as they huddled around Satan, whispering and looking my way.

Turning to look at Jesus, I was amazed to see angels appearing all around Him as well. Some were standing near Him on the ground, while others were hovering above Him. It was obvious they, too, had been looking on.

A soft, serious voice then spoke to me. "Becki, you have a decision to make. There isn't anyone here to influence you against your will. If you make the wrong choice, you will have no one to blame but yourself. You may never have this opportunity again."

Clearly, the time of decision had come. "Now, you can keep on living your life as you have been and let Satan be your god, or you can believe that Jesus really does love you and choose Him to be your God." After a pause, the invisible Being asked, "Becki, who do you want to be your god—Satan or Jesus?"

I didn't need a lot of time to think it over. My decision was made. I turned to Jesus, but He was gone!

11

The Ultimate Decision

Before I had a chance to panic, a voice said, "Look further ahead and look up higher."

A hill in the distance was wrapped in heavy, dark fog. A light was shining from a cross. As my eyes adjusted to the fog that was slowly dissipating, I could just make out Jesus' body hanging limply. I recognized the familiar symbol, but this time it was not just a symbol. I was there!

Many angels were crowded around the foot of the cross on the ground. They were distinctly different from the angels I saw above the cross. The angels on the ground were surrounded with dim light. A look of terror contorted their faces as they looked up at Jesus. Their heads were shaking slowly as they said, "Oh no. *Oh no. Oh no!*" The alarm in their voices increased each time they spoke. I sensed instantly what this meant. These angels were the ones who, by their influence, had brought about the killing of Jesus, and they seemed to know they had sealed their doom. Judgment Day was coming. Their fear was beyond description; they were clearly shaken.

Meanwhile, heaven's angels were high above the cross, looking down at the angels on the ground. They didn't speak to one another but, strangely, their thoughts were amplified in my mind. "You killed my best Friend! How could you do such a thing?" They were inconsolable. "*You killed my best Friend!*" One angel would reach out to hug another. Overwhelmed with grief, they wailed with deep, body-shaking sobs.

No words of comfort came to His angels from the limp body of Jesus. The spark of love I had seen flashing from His eyes was gone. His hair was matted with hardened clumps of congealed blood. I understood as never before that it was *my* sins that had put Him there.

I want Jesus. I'll go to Him. An irresistible longing drew me as I fixed my gaze upon Him. I began to walk toward Him, but a heavy weight pushed me onto my hands and knees. *I'll crawl to Him.* I barely managed to advance, but again that heavy weight pushed me flat onto my stomach.

Undeterred, I thought, *I'll pull myself like a snake on its belly if I have to—but I want Jesus!* With all my strength, I tried pulling myself forward, but the invisible weight was so heavy I was unable to move. At last, all I could do was lie on the ground and cry until there were no tears left.

If only I could be clean! If only I could be forgiven of all my sins, I thought, lifting my head and looking toward the cross. That is when I saw Jesus standing right in front of me—no longer on the cross. The darkness, grief, and pain of the cross was gone. Jesus had died for *my* sins.

He stood taller this time, as if He were my Father and I His young child. Responding to the love I saw in His eyes, I pulled myself up to my feet. *Whatever you do this time, Becki, don't take your eyes off of Him.* I was so afraid that I might blow this opportunity, I didn't wait for Jesus to speak to me.

"Jesus, I want to come to You, but I have too many sins." Intuitively I knew that it was my sins weighing me down and preventing me from going to Him.

"If You would, please come to me," I pleaded. "Would You please forgive me for all the sins I've done in my life, knowing they were wrong? I didn't care at the time, but I do care now, and I am sorry." But that wasn't enough. "And for all the sins I don't even know about," I continued. "Please forgive those too." I was determined to leave nothing unconfessed. I knew I didn't deserve His forgiveness or love, but the longing of my heart and soul came out in one last desperate cry: "Jesus, can I be Yours?"

Instantly I saw the heavens open and the angels in unrestrained celebration. Some angels jumped up and down, clapping their hands. Others fell to their knees with their hands raised high, waving their arms back and forth in front of the Father's throne. Angels ran to hug each other, weeping and singing their praises and hallelujahs aloud as they turned toward the Father's throne. I saw angels locking arms together in a flurry of ecstasy, leaping and twirling as they expressed their uninhibited joy.

"Wait! Wait!" Another angel motioned with his arm. All the angels became silent and focused their attention on the one who appeared to be their commanding angel. "He hasn't answered her yet."

In solemn silence, every eye turned to Jesus.

With downcast eyes, I waited for His answer. My heart pounded in my ears. Would He say, "I'd like to forgive you, but you've already had your chance, and it's too late now"? Or maybe, "I'd like to forgive you, but you have so many sins I can't forgive them all"? With a growing sense of doom, I wondered if I'd hear the words, "I'm sorry, but you've committed the unpardonable sin."

Anxiously I looked at Jesus, and as my eyes met His, I knew there was hope. He had been waiting for me to look at Him. His dark, beautiful eyes flashed with love and His voice caressed my soul. "I will," He whispered, though His whisper was majestic enough for everyone to hear it. "I forgive you."

Swiftly the head angel brought his arm downward as a signal for all of the angels to resume their celebration. Heaven's airwaves vibrated as the angels began praising the Father for the sacrifice of Jesus and for this one additional victory His death had accomplished.

Jesus knelt down in front of me. We were now eye-to-eye. He put both hands upon my shoulders. Tears filled His eyes and began to overflow as He pulled me in close to His heart and hugged me. We both were crying on each other's shoulders as He whispered to me, "You belong to Me now, and I will never let you go."

"I don't want You to let me go, Jesus," I said as I hugged Him tighter. "I don't ever want to go back where I was without You. I want to be Yours forever."

Over Jesus' shoulder, I saw Satan and his angels walking back into the trees. They were whispering to one another, casting parting looks our way. I could only imagine the plans they were making to get me back over to their side.

The dream ended. I found myself kneeling at my bed as I had been before the dream. I dried my eyes and smiled. *Yes. If Jesus were to come today, I would be ready.* This time I *knew* the dream was real. It was not my imagination. I had just stepped into a new beginning with Jesus as my Lord, Leader, and Guide for life. I was so overjoyed, I wanted to walk down Main Street and call out so everybody could hear, "Look out! Here comes a real, live Christian!"

In the midst of my euphoria, questions began to rise in my mind. *What exactly is a real, live Christian?* I asked myself. *Will I dress the same after this? How will I talk as a Christian? Jesus is my God, but what am I supposed to do now?*

I puzzled for only a moment before an idea clicked in my head. *Jesus is my God now. If anyone knows what I should do, it's Him.* His presence, so vivid to me in the dream, had lost none of its reality. Even though I couldn't *see* Him, I believed He was right there in the room with me. So I did the natural thing. I started talking to Him.

"Jesus, I don't know what to do now. Do I eat the same way? Dress the same way? Spend my money in the same way as I always have? If You had asked me to be a sinner, I could have done that with my eyes closed. But what do I do now as a Christian?" I was painfully aware of my inexperience and weakness.

The still, small Voice was unruffled. "Think about it, Becki. What is the one thing that all Christians claim to live by?"

That was easy! I got my Bible as Exodus 20 flashed into my mind. It took a while, but I found the Ten Commandments. *Now all I have to do is memorize them, and no matter where I'm at I'll always know how God wants me to live*, I reasoned.

From that moment, I started memorizing the Ten Commandments, hiding them in the recesses of my mind. If I could live to please the new Lord of my life, my happiness would be complete.

Things were going pretty well until I came to the fourth commandment. As I repeated the words of verses 9 and 10—"Six days you shall labor and do all your work, but the seventh day is the Sabbath of the Lord your God. In it you shall do no work"—I stopped short. I knew that Saturday was the seventh day of the week. I regularly worked from Friday night at midnight until eight in the morning on Saturday. Regretfully I realized that was a huge chunk of the Sabbath hours.

I began to strategize. *Couldn't I freshen up a bit after arriving home from work and go to church? No one would even know I had been up all night.* My first attempt at rationalizing began to deflate. *Well, no one would know except God—the very one I would be trying to hide it from.* I wryly shook my head, knowing that that plan was not going to work.

If I told my boss I didn't want to work on Friday nights or

Saturdays anymore, I was sure I could lose my job. Then what? But again I remembered my brand-new relationship. *I'll ask Jesus!*

Praying had me stumped when it came to using the accepted phrases and patterns of prayer, but talking to my best Friend, who was as near as my thoughts, was easy! So I just asked Him. Jesus was standing in front of me, listening intently.

"Jesus, what do You want me to do about my job?"

His voice was clear and reassuring. "I will be with you. I will take care of you and give you what you need in life. I will make you happy *if* you always look to Me, trust Me, and obey Me."

That sounded simple enough, but I continued to wrestle with reality.

"Jesus, I won't be able to pay my rent if I lose my job. I can't move back home, and I don't know where else I could go."

He repeated His answer with emphasis this time, "I *will* be with you. I *will* take care of you and *give* you what you need in life *if* you *always* look to Me, *trust* Me, and *obey* Me."

I don't know why it took me three times, but I finally got it. *If you're worrying, then you're not trusting. Do you believe Jesus or not?* I asked myself.

12

A Test of Faith

As I planned how I would request to take the Sabbath hours off from work, I knew there was something else I needed to take care of as well. In the glow of my new relationship with Jesus, I drove over to see my parents.

I walked in, sat down, and said these exact words: "I've just become a Christian. So from now on Jesus will be my God, not Satan." Mom's response was as sure and swift as my announcement had been.

"Well, Becki, I don't want anything to do with Jesus. And if that's what you want, then I don't want anything to do with you either." My own bluntness was now turned on me as Mom's agitation mounted. "I don't need anyone coming around here preaching at me or trying to shove any of that religious stuff down my throat. I don't want to hear it. I don't want anything to do with it." Even though I recognized whose spirit was speaking through her, the words stung my heart.

It had never occurred to me that my decision to make Jesus my God might mean the loss of my relationship with my own family. The painful thought that I might be the only one in my family that wanted Jesus or heaven was a crushing blow to my fragile new world.

But stoically I faced the possibility. *If it means I go to heaven alone, then that's what it means. I want Jesus more than anything or anyone. I will never go back to Satan!* I was determined.

Dad was sitting on the couch with his arm wrapped around Mom's waist. The expression on his face said something like, "Well, Becki, what are you going to do with that?"

Since I wasn't ready to accept life apart from my family, my work was cut out for me. I was already convinced that arguing wouldn't work. Wouldn't it be more convincing for them to see that life with Jesus was so much better than life with Satan? I was hoping that plan would help them want Jesus too.

"OK." I stood calmly to my feet. "I just wanted to let you know that from now on, I am a Christian."

My first day back at work arrived—the first workday after I'd decided to ask my boss to not schedule me on Friday nights or Sabbaths. In my personal devotions, I had begun to pray for God to grow my faith. He was about to answer that prayer.

As I came to the end of my night shift, I waited nervously in the main office for Mr. Blake, the head supervisor, to show up. He came in and reclined comfortably in his chair, sipping his coffee across from me. He was a pastor himself, but doubts began to rattle my nerve, and I turned my thoughts upward.

Jesus, You promised You would take care of me, I prayed silently. *Please help me say the right things. Help me trust You and obey You, even if I lose my job.*

My throat tightened as I let the words I had planned tumble out. "Mr. Blake, I've become a Christian on my days off, and from now on I'd like to keep the Sabbath holy to honor Jesus." He appeared to be pleased about my becoming a Christian, but he was processing the part about keeping the Sabbath.

Nervously I filled the empty space with my explanation. "The Bible says in Genesis, 'In the beginning God created the heavens and the earth.' It goes on to say, 'The evening and the morning were the first day,' and, 'The evening and the morning were the second day.' So according to the Bible, the seventh day, the Sabbath, begins in the evening on Friday and ends in the evening on Saturday. So I'd like to have Fridays and Saturdays off." I took a breath and added hopefully, "I'm willing to go back to the extra board if that will help."

The extra board was the list of newly hired workers. They were "extra" help in case someone called in sick. Being on the extra board would mean losing my seniority benefits and regular work hours.

Mr. Blake leaned forward, folded his hands on top of his desk, and said with an understanding smile, "I'll tell you what, Becki—I'll give you Friday nights and Saturdays off. If anyone calls in sick on your regularly scheduled nights off—Tuesday or Wednesday—we'll give you a call, and that way you can still get forty hours a week."

I felt weak with relief and replied, "Thank you, Mr. Blake."

On my way home, my heart was dancing with joy. Jesus had blessed me! I didn't lose my job. Everything was going to be OK.

That Friday evening as I stood watching the setting sun out my front window, I savored the realization that I didn't have to go to work. Little did I know Satan was organizing his countermove.

I planned to go to church on Sabbath morning, but what should I do tonight? I was alone in the apartment, because my girlfriend was hanging out with some of her friends. Remembering the Friday evenings I had spent with the youth group, I grabbed my guitar. Sitting down on the couch, I began strumming Christian songs we had sung together. Slowly the words came back, and by bedtime I was filled with peace.

The next morning, I arrived early at the Seventh-day Adventist church. In the foyer a woman greeted me warmly.

"May I talk with your pastor?" I asked.

She introduced us, and Pastor Jones reached out to shake my hand.

"Hi, I'm Becki. I've just become a Christian, and I'm ready to be baptized," I said in my usual, no-nonsense manner.

His eyes widened in surprise. "Oh?" Pastor Jones was momentarily speechless. "OK," he responded, recovering his voice. "I'd really like to get better acquainted first. Could we make an appointment for next week?"

"Sure," I agreed, a bit puzzled that he didn't plan to baptize me during the service that day. Oh well. I'd waited this long;

I should be able to wait until we talked. I was unaware of the preparation pastors typically make with baptismal candidates.

Back at work early Sunday morning, during one of my rounds as my night shift was winding down, I paused for a moment to enjoy the sunrise with the beautiful ice-cream-cone silhouette of Mount Saint Helens in the distance. In the early morning freshness, I reflected on my blessings. God had already worked things out so that I could keep my job without working on the Sabbath, and now I was looking forward to baptism! The future was lining up perfectly, until . . .

Satan appeared suddenly beside me wearing that shimmering sky-blue suit that I had seen him wear in my dream. He followed my gaze to the sunrise. "Do you really believe God has forgiven *all* of your sins?" At first, the words of doubt sent a cold chill down my spine. But God gave me courage, and I said, "Yes, I do believe God has forgiven all of my sins. The Bible says if I confess my sins to Him, He will forgive me and cleanse me of all my sins." My confidence in God's Word grew as I spoke. "I believe the Bible is true, and God doesn't lie." Just hearing myself say those words reaffirmed my new convictions. Satan vanished, but he had not given up.

When I got back to the main security office, I updated my relief officer for her shift and prepared to leave.

"Hey, Becki, wait a minute," Mr. Hendrix, who arranged the schedule, was looking at the extra board names and apparently evaluating his options. "We have a problem here, and I need you to work this coming Friday night."

Apprehension engulfed me as I stopped in the doorway and

looked back. "What?" I hoped I didn't look as concerned as I felt.

Mr. Hendrix explained that he had just received a phone call from a coworker who had to be out of town for a funeral. He began pointing to the names of those on the extra board.

"Scot's working at the east gate Friday night. Michelle will be working the shipping gate, and Brad will be on route B." He turned to face me. "You're the only one left who's qualified to fill in at the pulp gate. So I need you to work this Friday night."

Trembling, but with resolve, I said, "I'm sorry, Mr. Hendrix, but Mr. Blake has given me permission to have Friday nights off."

Mr. Hendrix's voice rose in frustration. "Well, if you don't come in this Friday, then I'll have to arrange this week's schedule all over again." I remained steadfast against his attempt to apply pressure.

"I'm sorry for this inconvenience, Mr. Hendrix, but Mr. Blake communicated with you about my schedule. He gave me permission to have Friday nights off, and I will not be here on Friday." I could see by his exasperated expression that my explanation wasn't convincing. "If you need me to help out on Tuesday or Wednesday nights, I'll be happy to come in," I offered. Then I left before he could raise any further arguments.

The next morning, I noticed that Mr. Hendrix had adjusted the schedule. Someone else would be filling in on Friday night. But instead of calling me to come in to work on either Tuesday or Wednesday night, he had scheduled others to work, which left me short on my hours for that week.

On Wednesday evening, Pastor Jones arrived at my apartment for a visit. "Oh, you've taken the Amazing Facts Bible studies and *The Bible Says* guides," he said as I showed him my collection. "Would it be OK with you if I took these home to read through them? I'd like to see how God has been leading in your life."

"Sure, OK." I shrugged.

He asked about my job, so I told him I was a security officer and that this past weekend had been my first Sabbath off.

"So, you have convictions about not working on the Sabbath?" he asked in surprise.

"Yes," I assured him. "I know the Bible teaches that the Sabbath is holy. I've made arrangements with my boss so I don't have to work during the Sabbath hours."

"That's good." He appeared to be thinking. "That's good."

We set a time for him to come back and visit again.

On the second visit, he told me, "I appreciate your honest responses in the study guides." He pulled out one of the Amazing Facts study guides and asked the question that was on the back.

"Are you ready for Jesus to come? Here's what you wrote at that time, Becki—'No, but I want to be.'" He looked up at me. "Your thoughtful answers tell me that you have been growing. And considering the fact that you have already been following your convictions about keeping the Sabbath holy without me even mentioning it—well, Becki, God has been leading in your life." With a smile he said, "It looks like you're ready for baptism."

13

Satan's Countermove

Those were welcome words for me. For nearly five years I had longed for this! Pastor Jones and I agreed to have one more visit before my baptism.

In his office the following week, we talked about all of the Seventh-day Adventist beliefs. He allowed me to ask any questions, and I did have one.

"It looks like you are a full-time pastor and that you don't have any other job on the side. So I'm curious about how you are able to survive. Surely the money comes from somewhere."

Pastor Jones explained that Seventh-day Adventists follow the model established for the Israelite nation during the time of Moses. "We call it the tithe system," he said. "As local church members, we acknowledge God's ownership and blessings, and we give one-tenth of our income, or tithe, and our freewill offerings at church. The tithe money is sent to the conference. The conference uses some of it to pay their pastors and other employees, similar to the way the priests in Israel were supported by the tithe collected in Bible times. The rest of the money is sent to the union, and it pays its employees. Then the union sends the remaining tithe to the North American Division, which does likewise on to the General Conference. The General Conference uses the tithe to pay pastors and other employees worldwide."

His answer satisfied my curiosity about how he was supported as a pastor. The well-ordered plan was simple and biblical, but for some reason at that time I didn't apply tithing to myself.

We set the date for my baptism about a month and a half away. Pastor Jones had a couple of others already scheduled to be baptized on that date, and I was happy to be another one joining in the baptism.

When the anticipated weekend finally arrived, it was meaningful to have my grandmother in the congregation, since she had introduced me to the Bible through her storytelling art. My roommate came as well.

As I stepped into the warm water, Pastor Jones placed my hands over his left wrist so I could hold on to his arm while going down into the water. He raised his right arm and said, "I now baptize you in the name of the Father and of the Son and of the Holy Spirit." As he did so, I was distracted by a form I saw through the skylight. An angel! My heart leaped. And then I saw another angel and another and another—the skylight was full of smiling angels crowding around to see my baptism!

Pastor Jones leaned me back. I felt the water fold over me, but as I came up to the surface, I thought, *You didn't hold me under long enough!* I had wanted the water to cover me as long as possible to ensure that I had been thoroughly washed clean from my past sins. But God gently soothed, "It's OK, Becki. I've got you covered."

Back at work, Mr. Harpster, one of the supervisors, had been asked to help Mr. Hendrix with the scheduling. I found that Mr. Harpster had placed me in another area of duty that paid about thirty cents fewer per hour and provided only about thirty hours of work a week. It became apparent that Mr. Harpster was trying to force me into weekend duty. But without complaint, I silently thanked God that I still had my job with the Sabbath hours off.

"Hey, Becki," Mr. Harpster commented one day, leaning back in his chair. "I can see that you stand pretty firm not working on Friday nights or Saturdays." Then with feigned concern on his face, he asked, "But what if we had an emergency? Would you leave us hanging if we really needed your help?"

This caught me by surprise. *Surely Jesus would help people in an emergency, wouldn't He?* I reasoned. I wanted to be like Jesus and for others to know that I cared about them.

"Well, I suppose if it were an emergency I would help. I'm sure Jesus would," I spoke hesitantly.

Something about Mr. Harpster's smile bothered me. "OK. I was just wondering." He swirled his chair around and went on about his business. I continued to write up my shift report in the record book.

Suddenly Mr. Harpster threw down his pencil in frustration. "OK, Becki, we have an emergency here." He looked at me with shrewd, crafty eyes. I instantly knew it had been a setup and that I had fallen for it.

Pointing out to me the different positions and the people who were working them, he made his plea. "Becki, you are the only one left who can work the main gate this Friday night. It's an emergency. We really do need your help here."

Like a cornered mouse, I felt trapped. "OK," I agreed, but I felt completely unsettled about the whole thing.

Still troubled when I got back to my apartment, I called Pastor Jones for advice. After I explained what had happened, he asked, "Have you worked any Sabbaths since you've become a Christian, Becki?"

"No," I answered. "But they keep trying to work things around to get me to come in on Sabbath."

Without exploring any possible compromises, he spoke straight and to the point. "OK, Becki. Tell your boss no—just as you have done since requesting Sabbath off. Tell him you cannot work this Friday night or any other Sabbath hours." His confident tone restored me to my original decision.

"Thank you, Pastor. I will." Though I was grateful for his support regarding this decision, I was shaken with the thought of reversing my answer and telling Mr. Harpster no. But it was the only answer I could give to keep my conscience clear with God.

The next night at work when I asked to speak with him, Mr. Harpster's keen eyes told me that he was expecting this conversation. I sent up a quick prayer for courage and guidance.

Then, ignoring my fears, I dove in.

"Mr. Harpster, I know I told you I would come in to work this Friday night, but after further consideration I've changed my mind. I'm not comfortable going against my convictions about the Sabbath."

"OK." He threw his hands up in the air as a show of accepting my resolve, but I didn't miss the suspicious twinkle in his eye. "I'll see what I can do."

He looked at the schedule and made a couple of phone calls. "Got it!" He said to himself triumphantly as he hung up the phone. "Don't worry, Becki. I've got it solved." He had a strategy all right, but was it in my best interest? I wasn't so sure. Though I was honoring God by keeping the Sabbath, it appeared that Mr. Harpster was going to make me pay somehow.

I'd developed the habit of taking my Bible to work, so I could read during the quiet times. In doing that I had come across the book of Malachi. " 'Bring all the tithes into the storehouse, that there may be food in My house, and try Me now in this,' says the LORD of hosts, 'if I will not open for you the windows of heaven and pour out for you such blessing that there will not be room enough to receive it'" (Malachi 3:10). I paused, remembering Pastor Jones's explanation about how the tithe supported the ministers. But did God really expect me to be faithful with tithing when my drop in weekly hours had resulted in earning less money?

Patiently God allowed me time to think things through. Though the passage's serious tone was frightening to me, I was impressed with the promise it carried. Now it appeared to me that I should return the tithe, no matter how unreasonable it seemed. This processing and questioning lasted for a number of days. I continued reading my Bible and looking for answers.

In the meantime, Mount Saint Helens was beginning to rumble. The forestry department had asked for extra help in the main office reporting the seismic activity to the men working in the red zone. They needed people to work the swing shift and night shift during the week and around the clock on the weekends. We had about two hundred security officers, but only eight of us were qualified for that position. I was one of them.

Mr. Hendrix chose five of the eight to be trained by Brianna, the head of the forestry department. I was one of the five. Three days of training were followed by another three days of unsupervised work before Brianna would choose three of us to help her during this time of need.

Brianna was a Christian, and we got along quite well. After my six days were up, I'd finished with the night shift, and Brianna came in to work the day shift. We sat laughing and talking as usual before I headed home. Then she casually asked me, "Well, Becki, what do you think of the forestry department? It appears that you've done a pretty good job here. Is this something you'd like to do part-time to help us out?" It was a relaxed atmosphere, so I spoke candidly, not knowing where things were leading.

14

Faith Wins

"There's no way I would want this job part-time," I said bluntly.

Brianna blinked a couple of times, taken aback by my response. But she pressed me, "Would you mind telling me why?"

"This job is way too serious for me to do it part-time. I couldn't possibly be prepared to make life-and-death decisions in seconds during an emergency if I came in here only once every few weeks. If I made mistakes, it could cost a lot of men working in the red zone their lives." I paused, shaking my head slowly. "People are valuable, and the only way I'd want this job is if I could do it full-time—not part-time."

Brianna smiled. "Well, that makes sense, Becki. I see what you mean."

With my training behind me, I returned to my regular schedule in my booth at the plant site. The scripture in Malachi 3 was still working its way into my thoughts, and conviction was strongly settling in. I had started returning 10 percent tithe on my weekly paycheck. My first month of tithing was coming to an end.

Grabbing a piece of paper, I began subtracting 10 percent tithe, then rent, gas, food, and other essentials. By the time I'd finished all my subtracting, the balance was clear—my wages didn't cover my expenses. In my frustration I stood up on a chair and pressed the paper on which I had scribbled my figures high up in the window. It was dark and raining outside, so I imagined God's vision could be obstructed, and I was determined to get as close to heaven as I could. There in the privacy of my work booth, with no one else around to see what I was doing, I spoke to Him.

"Look at this!" I addressed God without inhibition, notifying Him of my need. "I know Your math is better than mine, but this just doesn't add up. They've been changing my schedule and putting me in different places that give me less pay. They're trying to get me to come in and work on Friday nights. Now the end of the month is coming, and I won't have enough to pay my rent for the next month." I paused, giving my reason a chance to catch up with my passion. After all, I was addressing the great God of the universe who loved me. I took a deep breath as my racing heart slowed. "You *promised* me that if I obeyed You, You would take care of me. I'm in trouble here. Something has to change." With the tirade over, I plopped myself down in my chair, not knowing what else to do.

A quiet, kind voice spoke into my thoughts. "Becki, has it ever occurred to you that God is testing you to see whether you really trust Him to take care of you?"

That was a new thought. It never crossed my mind that God was watching *me* to see how much I trusted *Him*.

I dabbed at my eyes and said, "OK, I give You my word. No matter what happens to me, I will not work *any* Sabbath." My voice had softened by now. "You promised to take care of me. If I lose this job"—I expressed the unthinkable and then continued—"You must have another one for me somewhere else. *I believe Your promise!*" The last four words were punctuated with feeling. And it felt good to hear myself say them.

No sooner had I sat down than Mr. Hendrix arrived. I could tell by the way he slammed the door of his security truck that something was up. He blew into my booth and his angry eyes threatened to burn through me.

"I don't know what you told Brianna, but she called me and told me she wanted you to work for her. I tried to object because I'd have to rearrange the entire forestry schedule since you refuse to work on Friday nights," he raged. "She told me, 'I don't care if you have to rearrange everyone's schedule on the entire plant site. I want her up here starting this Sunday night with forty hours a week, and you make sure you give her the Sabbath hours off,' and then she hung up on me!" Sizzling hot, he whipped out a piece of paper.

"So here's your new schedule." He shoved the paper at me. "You'll be working in the forestry department starting this

Sunday night." Was it my imagination, or did I see steam billowing out from under his security hat? "You'll have forty hours a week with Friday and Saturday nights off."

I was in shock to see this macho man ordered to go against his will.

"Can she do that?" I asked.

He turned his piercing gaze on me to let me know just how naive I really was. "Yes, she can do that!" He waved his hand in exasperation, and his tone of voice rose higher. "She's a Weyerhaeuser employee. If I don't do what she says, the whole security company is fired—there goes not only my job, but my boss's job as well!" He reached into his attaché case and pulled out another piece of paper. "Here are the wages she demanded that you get paid."

In a quick glance, I was surprised to see I had just received a raise of one dollar and thirty-six cents an hour! *Wow, I knew God could take care of me, but I didn't know He'd do it this fast*, I thought. And God's job was so complete, Mr. Hendrix tried to get me to come in on Friday night only one more time.

It was Friday evening when I received a phone call from him. He explained that Diane had a family emergency and couldn't come in. "Becki, this is serious, and it really is an emergency. I promise I won't ever ask you to come in again if you'll help me out just this one time." He paused, waiting for my response.

God had shown me clearly through His miraculous means that I should honor Him by keeping the Sabbath holy. I was unbending.

"I'm sorry Mr Hendrix. I really *can't* come in during the Sabbath hours."

"Please, Becki," he began again, giving it his best shot, "can't you get special permission from your pastor just this once? Please, I *really* need your help."

"You don't understand, Mr. Hendrix." I explained calmly but firmly. "My pastor doesn't have the authority to tell me it's OK to disobey God." I was surprised at what I'd just heard myself say. After a moment of stunned silence, Mr. Hendrix spoke in almost a whisper. "I see. OK. I, uh, I guess I'll just have to do this job myself. Thanks, Becki."

He did cover for Diane that night, and never again was I pressured to work during the Sabbath hours.

It had been a wonderful evening at church. It was Halloween night, but our church social had no resemblance to the Halloweens of my childhood. It had just been a pleasant social time, reflecting what could have been any Saturday night of the year.

On a happy impulse, I decided to stop by my parents' place on my way home. But as I stepped through the front door I immediately realized I had made a mistake. Mom was sitting on the sofa with the Ouija game on her lap while my younger brother, sister, cousin, and a family friend were looking on with great interest. *What else would they be doing on Halloween night?* I thought wryly.

A spirit, tall and slender in a long overcoat, was standing beside Mom. He looked like the same spirit who had dumped my aunt's coffee onto the floor years earlier. His left hand was resting on Mom's right shoulder, and his right hand was placed over the top of her hand, moving the message indicator along. *Oh, that's how it works*, I thought with sudden awareness.

I was still standing near the front door, observing the scene, when Mom commanded, "Becki, leave!"

"It won't work for you, will it, Mom?" I couldn't resist the teasing remark. By now I well knew that the spirits hated the Bible just as they hated the Christians who believed it. They had refused to talk to Mom for several years after Randy had put the Bible on top of the game board. A Christian in the room had to be very disturbing to them.

"Becki, *leave!*" The increased volume in her voice accentuated the hostility behind her words. Mom's rudeness made our family friend, Felicia, feel confused.

"Why? What's wrong?" she asked. "We're just playing an innocent game."

I ignored her questions and looked straight at Mom. I wanted to make a difference for Jesus. So once again I said, "It won't work for you, will it, Mom?"

I saw the spirit lean over and whisper something in Mom's ear. She flashed me a look that let me know I was in serious trouble. Whenever she got that look in her eye, supernatural strength would come upon her. Immediately I sensed the presence of another being right beside me, whispering in my ear.

"Becki, I know you came in here in innocence; but I never stay where I'm not wanted, so we're leaving. If you choose to stay, you're on your own." Feeling the presence of God and His angel pulling away from me, I turned on my heels and ran out the door with them. I knew I was no match for the wily devil.

I drove away, and my family's Halloween party continued without me. Though I was disappointed in Mom's response that night, I didn't realize how Jesus' true love, which never forces itself on others, was even now drawing her heart to Him.

15

Unexpected Love

Though wrapped up in my newfound faith, I couldn't help noticing two tall, good-looking brothers at church. After all, we were involved in the same youth group. Fourteen of us would get together on Friday evenings to have Bible discussions on various topics we were interested in. Kevin played the guitar, and Steve played a great banjo for our singing sessions.

I had a growing admiration for them from afar, but they stayed to themselves as did I. However, in time, even the worst case of shyness weakens. As we spent Sabbath afternoons going for hikes in the mountains or walking on the beach in the summertime, we were really connecting and enjoying one another's company. In the winter, sometimes we'd play table games after sundown on Saturday.

On one of these evenings, I asked to play Kevin's guitar. He looked surprised. "You play the guitar?"

"Yes, I play some," I said as he handed it to me. I began to strum a melody. He and Steve exchanged smiles as they listened.

"Can you play 'Wildwood Flower'?" Steve asked with a twinkle in his eye.

"Sure." I nodded, transitioning into the country tune. I didn't know it then, but that song was a ticket into Steve's heart. It led to an invitation to join his family's jam sessions, where I met his other brothers, Randy, who played the bass guitar, and Ron, who played the mandolin. Surrounded by all that country and bluegrass music, I thought I was in heaven!

Still getting acquainted with some of the cultural expressions in Adventism, I asked Steve one day, "What's this ABC I keep hearing about?"

"Oh, it stands for Adventist Book Center," he explained. "It's a store that has all kinds of Bibles, books, and music—stuff like that."

After the next youth group meeting, as a careful disguise for a date, Steve asked, "Hey, Becki, I'm going to the ABC this week—would you like to check it out?"

"Sure," I smiled, "I'd love to go with you. I'm interested in seeing what it's like." Disguise or not, I was pleased he'd asked.

But books and Bibles were not the only thing the store carried. As Steve was making his purchases, I came to the food section. I recognized bags of nuts, different kinds of beans, and bags of dried fruit, but something else caught my eye. I picked up a can just as Steve joined me.

"What's this?" I held up the can with a picture of a mouth-watering meat loaf on the label.

"Oh, these are vegetarian meats," Steve motioned to the shelves of cans. "Many Adventists don't eat meat. So these are alternatives that have been developed to take the place of meat."

Curious, I purchased a couple of cans to try. Back in my apartment, I opened a can to add to my spaghetti sauce and examined the mixture. *You've got to be kidding me!* I continued to stare at the substance. It looked suspiciously like dog food. I sniffed at it, wondering if I should throw it away.

But, deciding to solve this mystery, I dumped it in the spaghetti sauce and was pleasantly surprised with the result. Having gone vegetarian years ago, I continued to taste and experiment with other canned vegetarian meat substitutes.

"Hey," Steve said one evening as our meeting was breaking up, "would you like to meet a couple who are interested in studying the Bible?" I didn't know it then, but Steve had a growing interest in giving Bible studies.

We met Greg and Patty, a friendly elderly couple who were excited we had stopped by. What fun we had every time we visited after that! They had a lighthearted sense of humor and were full of questions. Patty loved to cook and always had some new recipe she'd whipped up for us to sample.

As time went on, Steve and I spent a lot of time together—whether it was giving Bible studies, playing music together, or hanging out with other young friends in the church.

One day Steve brought me home after a Bible study. I had been pondering just what the Lord had in mind for me. I figured Steve, as another young adult, had asked himself that question too. "What do you think God has planned for us?" I asked as he cut the ignition.

His ready response took me by surprise. "Well, it must be something *together*." He looked earnestly at me. "I mean, look at the way everything has worked out for us this far. It all just seems so natural that we will continue *together*."

My heart couldn't deny his logic as the conversation turned toward marriage. We agreed to talk with our pastor. He met with us several times. During our sessions, he shared practical advice as well as spiritual insights. We were able to see some areas of challenge we would certainly have, but overall, each session only served to increase our conviction that God had brought us together and meant for our relationship to be permanent. It seemed the natural thing for us to follow God's leading, and we committed our lives to each other in marriage.

After settling into my new life as Mrs. Rogers, I stopped to visit with Mom one day. It was just the two of us. As we talked about nothing in particular, she asked, "Does God really forgive people who've done something wrong? Is He really that merciful?"

I had made a promise to myself that I would never "preach" at my family, but she was asking, and well—that was different! With my heart racing in eagerness I said, "Mom, the Bible says that God is love. Everything about God is love." How I wanted her to know this God! "There's no sin so horrible or bad that Jesus can't forgive if we want to be forgiven." She leaned toward me as I spoke. "Jesus sacrificed His life in order to give sinners another chance and to get them into His kingdom in heaven," I assured her.

Though I didn't know what was going on in her mind, I sensed that she was really interested in being free from Satan's grasp. I was sure God was working with her heart and wanted to give her victory, while at the same time Satan was in a panic. Realizing the door of salvation was cracking open for her, I felt impressed to push it further with the choice God was giving her.

"Mom, you know all this spiritualistic stuff isn't good. Why don't you get rid of it?" I waited as she twisted her hair through her fingers.

"I don't have enough room in my garbage can. I have only one." Her words were flat and emotionless. I could tell she was just making excuses.

"That's no problem, Mom," I said in what I hoped was a calm, accommodating voice. "I have plenty of room in the garbage at my place. I can take it all for you."

She continued to twirl her hair through her fingers. I could only imagine how she was struggling with the idea of letting go of all of the things that had been so meaningful to her.

"No, I wouldn't want you to bother with it."

Though she appeared noncommittal, I felt confident that she was in the midst of a spiritual battle. I couldn't bear to see her lose this opportunity to choose God's side.

"Mom, you're listening to the wrong voice," I asserted boldly. "That's Satan talking to you. He doesn't want you to give up that stuff." With every ounce of convincing urgency I could muster, I continued, "I'm telling you the truth. God *loves* you, and He can forgive you and help you let go. Listen to God's voice, Mom." I paused. *Will she yield?* "Won't you let me take all of your satanic stuff and get rid of it?"

My words hung in the air for a brief moment. Then she smiled serenely. "OK, you can take it."

Like a bullet, I leaped from the couch, dashed upstairs, and brought down several armloads of her satanic encyclopedias, magazines, tarot cards, and other spiritualistic items. There was no time to lose; I didn't want to risk Mom changing her mind.

As Mom watched, I began ripping up her encyclopedias. I invited her to join me. At first, she declined, but I encouraged her again.

"Here's one you can tear up if you'd like to help me," I offered. After hesitating briefly, she grabbed the book and began tearing out pages and ripping them in half. Flashing a childlike smile, she continued her enthusiastic tearing until that book was no more.

I handed her another and another until all the books and magazines were torn to pieces. By now, I had three large trash bags full of her stuff.

"You know, I still owed more than $500 on those books," she mentioned as she nodded toward the black bags. I had no idea that she'd been making payments on those books. It was mind-boggling to me. *What a mighty victory for Jesus*, I thought.

"Mom, what about your Ouija board?" I held my breath, knowing that this was her primary source for communicating with the spirits.

"OK, you can take it too." She motioned with her hand toward the bedroom, giving me permission to go get it. I ran into her room, grabbed it from the top of her closet, and brought it into the living room. She appeared relaxed and content as I broke it up and put it in one of the bags.

When the bulging bags were securely tied, we sat in silence, savoring this life-changing moment before I carried the trash bags to my car and drove to County Line State Park. Bringing the bags over to one of the firepits, I began to burn the materials that had kept Mom tied to Satan. While the fire blazed, I looked up into the clouds. A few stars were beginning to twinkle in the darkening sky. A sweet peace engulfed me, and I felt lifted a little closer to heaven.

Opening my heart in prayer, I said, "Lord, I don't have anything of significant value to offer you. I just give you myself. If You can use me in any way, I'm available. You can use me however You'd like."

It was a simple prayer, but I meant it. I had no idea what God had in store for me. I only knew I wanted my life to be pleasing to Him.

Now that I was away from home with its demonic manifestations and growing in my knowledge of Jesus as my personal Savior and Friend, I literally relaxed. Keeping my Bible close and being always aware of my guardian angel, my sleep became sweet and refreshing.

Knowing all of my sins were forgiven and washed away gave me so much joy. I now had a reason to live. No longer was my goal to get as much stuff from this world as I could. Rather, I lived to please Jesus and spent each day enjoying all the blessings that heaven has to offer. I was experiencing heaven in the present and looked forward to it in its fullness when Jesus returns and opens the Holy City's gates for all who love Him.